SWIM SWIM

A COMPLETE HANDBOOK FOR FITNESS SWIMMERS

KATHERINE VAZ AND CHIP ZEMPEL
WITH THE EDITORS OF *SWIM SWIM* MAGAZINE

CONTEMPORARY
BOOKS, INC.
CHICAGO ▪ NEW YORK

Library of Congress Cataloging-in-Publication Data

Vaz, Katherine.
  Swim, swim.

    Includes index.
    1. Swimming.   2. Swimming—Training   I. Zempel,
Chip.   II. Title
GV837.V37   1986   797.2'1   85-23279
ISBN 0-8092-5134-5

Photos by Harald Johnson

Copyright © 1986 by Katherine Vaz and the Editors of *Swim Swim* Magazine
All rights reserved
Published by Contemporary Books, Inc.
180 North Michigan Avenue, Chicago, Illinois 60601
Manufactured in the United States of America
Library of Congress Catalog Card Number: 86-23279
International Standard Book Number: 0-8092-5134-5

Published simultaneously in Canada by Beaverbooks, Ltd.
195 Allstate Parkway, Valleywood Business Park
Markham, Ontario L3R 4T8 Canada

CONTENTS

1
LAST ONE IN'S A ROTTEN EGG!

Americans have grown so accustomed to seeing people running and bicycling through their neighborhoods, many of us are surprised to discover that polls and surveys consistently rank *swimming* as America's number one fitness sport in terms of participation. Not only are more and more people swimming in the ever-increasing number of backyard and community pools, but athletes from other sports are finding swimming a great way to maintain their conditioning during the off-season, rehabilitate injuries, and improve their flexibility. And the fastest-growing competitive sport—the *triathlon*—is swelling swimming's ranks even more as runners and cyclists discover the joys and benefits of cross-training.

On the other hand, few of these swimmers are aware of how much the sport has changed in the last two decades. Not only have major innovations occurred in the ways that swimmers train and compete, but fundamental notions of what propels the swimmer through the water and how the strokes should be performed have been completely revamped. Several years ago the President's Council on Physical Fitness and Sports predicted there would be thirty-nine million adult swimmers by

*Last one in's a
rotten egg!*

1988, but the authors of this book predict that many of them will be swimming with "horse-and-buggy technique" in today's electronic age.

Are you swimming more now but enjoying it less? Has your initial enthusiasm become tarnished as your weight loss slowed down and finally leveled off, leaving you with those last few pounds you just can't seem to shed?

Have your times stopped improving, leaving you frustrated and wondering how the people in other lanes can be going faster while taking fewer, not to mention *slower*, strokes? Do you suspect that your technique needs improvement but don't know where to start or how to begin?

Maybe you've gotten to the point where you hardly even notice your swimming any more. Has it just become another daily chore: go down to the pool, switch on the timer and automatic pilot, get out, shower, and go to work? Maybe you're new to swimming and excited about the whole prospect of swimming being your number-one route to health and beauty (or any of the thousands of other reasons we exercise), and you want to get started on the right foot. Perhaps you're an athlete from another sport, a runner with shin splints or back problems, or a cyclist with chondromalacia whose doctor recommended swimming as a way to keep in shape while you recover from your injuries. Or are you a triathlete, looking for tips that will improve your split on the swimming leg?

Whatever your reasons for swimming, you wouldn't have read this far if you weren't interested in improvement. That's what this book is all about. Here's a taste of just a few of the things you can expect to find in this book.

We'll begin by shattering some of the old myths and wives' tales surrounding the sport. Then we'll take a look at what the exercise physiologists have discovered about swimming technique with their ultra-high-speed movie cameras and computerized motion analyses of World Champions and Olympic Gold Medalists, and how they've changed our most fundamental notions of what propels a swimmer through the water. And we'll show you how their findings affect *your* swimming. We'll also look at discoveries modern psychology has made about learning and brain function and give some pointers on how to learn these new techniques more quickly and easily.

We'll show you some of the tricks that swimmers and coaches use to make their workouts more efficient, effective, and entertaining and take a look at training aids, pool etiquette, and getting the most out of your swimming time.

Then we'll move on to a discussion of training, how workouts are designed to achieve specific goals, and how to design your own workouts. For those of you who get an itch every now and then to test yourself and measure your progress, we'll take a look at competition, with an emphasis on the *fun* events and the least intimidating ways for beginners to ease themselves into this special and rewarding world.

Finally, we'll attempt to lure you from your concrete swimming holes into the outside. Runners and cyclists would go insane if they had to circle a track exclusively, yet the vast majority of swimmers never experience the thrill and challenge of swimming in open water. We'll show you how to prepare for a safe and enjoyable excursion into this whole new world. But we should warn you: you might become addicted!

WHY SWIMMING?

The psychological benefits of exercise have received lots of publicity in recent years. Exercise does give one a sense of relaxation and well-being, and swimming may be better at this than most other sports. Psychologists theorize that rolling back and forth in a liquid environment and feeling weightless remind us of the womb, a time when everything was good and all our needs were met. Some even suggest that water calls forth a deep unconscious memory of all life having its beginnings in the sea. Whatever the reason, water does have a special attraction for many. Bodies of water, from a humble creek or abandoned quarry to a mighty ocean, are favorite places to "get away from it all."

For the fledgling U.S. space program in the 1950s, research was done on the psychological effects of long periods of time with little sensory input. When volunteers were placed in flotation tanks in totally dark, soundproofed laboratories, psychologists expected brain activity to shut down in the absence of external stimulation. To their surprise, just the opposite happened. Many of the volunteers reported very rich and vivid sensory experiences, similar to accounts of people who had taken psychedelic drugs.

Swimmers often slip into a similar "sensory deprivation" trance, especially those who swim for prolonged periods of time. The silence, the monotonous visual surroundings, the steady rhythm of the stroke and kick, the sense of weightlessness—how hypnotic it can be. Some people even refer to their daily swim as their "meditation."

You may have also read about a class of substances known as *endorphins*, a sort of narcotic produced by the brain in response to strenuous exercise. These chemicals have received credit (or blame, depending on your point of view) for the "runner's high" or "second wind" phenomenon, the feeling of euphoria many athletes experience during and after a good workout. They may also be responsible for the "positive addiction" that makes athletes tense and crabby when they don't get their regular "fix" of exercise.

Reseachers have identified another factor that causes the brain to release endorphins in even higher amounts than exercise does—cold. Perhaps this is why rough-water swimmers often report such an intense euphoria after they swim in the open—they're getting a double dose of endorphins.

On the physical side, you're probably already aware that regular swimming produces physiological changes associated with any prolonged aerobic exercise—improved cardiovascular fitness, a lower resting heart rate, higher volumes of blood pumped per beat, reduced blood pressure, and so on—but swimming also has some of its own advantages. For example, since you are horizontal in the water, your heart doesn't have to pump against gravity. This makes it ideal for people who are seriously out of shape or have circulatory problems. Also, because of a phenomenon know as the "mammalian diving reflex," swimming causes humans to automatically breathe more deeply than other sports. Swimming has one of the lowest injury rates of any sport, and it's often recommended for the elderly, people with osteoporosis, and those with injuries of joints or connective tissue from other sports.

2
TEN SWIMMING MYTHS

Every sport has its legendary tales. Old-timers in San Francisco like to talk of the days when Alcatraz Island was still a prison and the guards would fire over the heads of swimmers racing in the bay for fun. Olympic champion Johnny Weissmuller was rumored to hold a little back whenever he swam because he received money under the table when he broke one of his own records, and wonderful stories circulate of how fast he really could swim when he wanted to.

Whether these stories are true or not, they add a touch of charm and romance to the sport. But, like the story of the bogeyman, there are other myths that we all need to outgrow sooner or later, and we want to take a look at some of them with you. Though it may seem heretical, we're going to start off with a biggie.

MYTH #1—SWIMMING IS THE BEST ALL-AROUND EXERCISE

Of course, everyone likes to think that his or her sport is the best, but somehow swimmers have managed to stake this

Swimming's one of the best all-around exercises.

claim more convincingly than participants in other sports.

Part of this claim can be traced to a sub-myth, the assumption that swimming is "total body exercise," working your arms and legs equally. Unfortunately, that's true only if you are doing it wrong! Research has shown that the butterfly, backstroke, and freestyle (or crawl) rely almost entirely on the upper body for propulsion, while kicking serves only to maintain correct body position.

Of course, regular swimming does provide the improved cardiovascular fitness we discussed earlier—higher stroke volume and lower resting heart rate, reduced blood pressure, and so on—and very few injuries are associated with the sport.

It's also a very gentle way to improve flexibility. In addition we've seen how swimmers may reap a greater share of the relaxation, reduced tension, and enhanced self-esteem that are typical psychological benefits of exercise.

While swimming certainly is *one* of the best exercises, it does have several drawbacks, not the least of which is that you have to *learn* how to do it and then find a pool somewhere. Lacing up a pair of jogging shoes and stepping out the front door is a lot less hassle.

But besides that, did you know that swimmers are notorious for having poor balance and that swimming is one of the *lowest*-rated sports for developing the kind of muscle definition that seems to be so fashionable nowadays? (Those hunks you saw at the last Olympics got that way from lifting weights, not swimming!)

Swimming also involves such a specialized pattern of movements that athletes often develop front-to-back muscle imbalance resulting in "swimmer's slouch," and several types of joint and muscle problems can be traced to these imbalances. As a matter of fact, one good reason for swimmers to lift weights is to strengthen those muscles *not* used by swimming.

On the psychological side, we mentioned the almost hypnotic trance many swimmers experience.

As beautiful as it sounds, this dreamy, peaceful state can actually become a *hindrance* to someone intent on getting into shape and becoming faster.

So what is the best all-around exercise? Who knows? Maybe the best one is any one that keeps you interested in exercising. So if you've decided that swimming is the best exercise for you, you're probably right.

MYTH #2—SWIMMING IS THE BEST WAY TO LOSE WEIGHT

While it is true that an effective weight-loss program must include exercise, swimming isn't really ideal. This is because, while most types of exercise, especially running, cause appetite suppression, swimming can actually *enhance* the appetite. Watch a bunch of runners after a race, sipping on their water bottles filled with Gatorade and munching on raisins or granola. Where are the swimmers? Driving around looking for a pizzeria or ice-cream parlor!

As we have just mentioned, swimming doesn't rank high on creating muscle definition, either. This means that if you were to compare a runner, an aerobic dancer, and a swimmer, with all three having exactly the same proportions of body fat, the swimmer would *look* softer and less muscular.

However, we have also discussed several reasons why swimming may be the best choice for *you*, and there's no reason why you can't swim off those extra pounds if you prefer that to pounding asphalt around your neighborhood or leaping about your living room to the latest celebrity exercise video.

On the contrary, because the swimmer is supported by water, it may be ideal for someone who is extremely overweight. This weightless feeling, and the fact that the exercise can be eased into gradually with so little intensity or strain on the heart, can be very encouraging to someone who is just beginning a weight-loss program.

If you are swimming to lose weight, let's review some basic principles:

Rule number one: There's no such thing as spot reduction. People may think they're seeing results, but what is actually happening is that the muscles underneath the fat are being toned up—the fat's still there. Fat follows a "first on, last off" rule. The biggest bulges are the last to go.

Rule number two: You must combine dieting and exercise for healthy, permanent weight loss. If you diet only, you'll lose a pound of muscle for every pound of fat you lose. Since muscle is much harder to gain back, you are worse off than when you started. Exercising while you diet preserves the muscle, making your body burn only fat.

Rule number three: Don't worry about your weight; worry about what *percentage* of that weight is fat. There are sophisticated ways of measuring fat with calipers or underwater weighing, but you can tell a lot by just pinching and looking in the mirror. Pinch the skin around your waist, inside your thighs, under your arms, and at the side of your pectoralis chest muscles. Is there fat under that skin? (For more information on losing weight, see Chapter Four.)

Rule number four: Short bursts of energy, sprinting, or

lifting weights for just a few repetitions don't use fat for fuel. Fat is a slow-burning fuel, and you need a prolonged period of aerobic exercise to mobilize it and burn it. The section on Target Heart Rates in Chapter Five, "Starting Out," will show you how to determine the proper level of exercise. If you're very overweight and out of shape, be careful to ease into your program gradually.

Rule number five: Weight control is a matter of changing your lifestyle. Swimming is a wonderful lifetime sport that can help.

MYTH #3—DON'T EAT OR DRINK ANYTHING FOR AT LEAST AN HOUR BEFORE SWIMMING

. . . or you'll get a stomach cramp and die!

What will it take to lay this one to rest? You've probably heard amazing tales about marathon runners loading up on pasta the night before a race and pancakes the next morning. Marathon swimmers do the same thing. As a matter of fact, in any event that lasts more than three hours, it becomes mandatory for the athlete to replace fluids, minerals, and some carbohydrates in order to keep going.

On the other hand, if you really gorge yourself or fill up with ice-cold beverages right before exercising, you may get sick to your stomach no matter what sport it is. But if you've eaten a normal meal, you don't have to sit on the pool deck waiting for that hour to tick by.

You sweat any time your body becomes overheated— swimmers sweat like anybody else. It's just not as noticeable. As odd as it may sound, dehydration can be a serious problem for swimmers. If you find yourself feeling very tired toward the end of a tough workout, especially when the water's hot, try drinking some water. You may be surprised at how much it can help.

Even though they aren't much of a tradition in swimming, we'd like to remind everyone that salt tablets are very danger-ous. They can actually cause your body to lose even *more* salt than it's losing already. In other words, they can kill you. Don't take them!

Lap swimming doesn't have to be boring.

MYTH #4—SWIMMING IS BORING AND MONOTONOUS

Anyone who has swum in the ocean, miles from shore, in six-foot seas, will tell you that it isn't boring. Nor is swimming in an emerald mountain lake when you can still see snow on the surrounding peaks (brrrr!). Or standing on a beach with hundreds of other swimmers when the sun is just beginning to color the sky, seeing a white flare waggling up into the dark sky—one minute to the start!

How about traveling to another country to participate in the Masters World Games, meeting other athletes who don't speak your language but understand you all the same? Or knowing that the next Masters National Championships will be held in your part of the United States, and that anyone— even *you*—can participate. Or just stepping up on the starting blocks at a local meet, seeing the official raise his pistol, and hearing him announce, "One hundred yards of freestyle. . . . Take your marks!"

But what about the everyday back-and-forth, you say? Even everyday workouts can—and *should*—be fun. One of the signs of a good coach is creativity, the ability to keep swimmers motivated, challenged, and entertained. Swimming isn't boring, but some workouts are.

Add variety to your swimming. Break the swims into shorter swims, swim different strokes, or build your speed from fast to slow within each swim or on successive ones. Practice your *worst* stroke for a change, or your worst kick.

Another thing that can keep swimming interesting and fun is the camaraderie that can develop. Get to know the people at workouts, and when you go to a meet, find out who those other swimmers are. Friendships formed at swimming meets are unique relationships, and many of us look forward to competing because of the social interaction as much as anything else.

Boredom can also be a signal that your interest and enthusiasm are waning. The most effective way of preventing this is to set *goals* for yourself, to challenge yourself to make those goals. Then measure your progress regularly. For instance, if you want to swim 500 yards in a certain time, figure out what your time has to be for each 100 yards. Then, once every week or two, swim a set of five 100s, taking as much rest in between as you want, trying to bring your time for each one down to that goal time. When you can finally hold that time for all five, start shortening your rest or try to do three 200s at twice your 100 time. Eventually, you'll reach your goal and it will be time to find a new challenge.

The secret to preventing boredom is keeping yourself motivated by finding new goals, new challenges, and then planning and measuring your progress toward them.

MYTH #5—YOU NEED TO SWIM ONLY THREE TIMES A WEEK FOR AEROBIC IMPROVEMENT

This is only partly true. Doctors recommend a minimum of twenty minutes of aerobic exercise at least three times a week to maintain a healthy cardiovascular system. Exercising for this amount will safely bring someone who is out of shape up to a minimum level of fitness.

But that's about all it will do. Once a person's body adapts to this level of training, the improvement begins to taper off and our new athlete reaches that most frustrating obstacle, a plateau. The exercise is no longer challenging, and as the body stops adapting, the person stops seeing signs of improvement—faster times, better endurance—and begins to go stale.

There are three ways to get off one of these plateaus: exercise more often, or for a longer period of time, or at higher intensity. The best method, the one that's most interesting, enjoyable, and challenging, is to combine a little of all three.

MYTH #6—TO GET IN SHAPE FAST, YOU HAVE TO SWIM FAST

If you are in poor shape to begin with, maximum efforts can put an enormous strain on the heart and circulatory system. In other words, this myth can *kill* you!

Long, slow distance (or LSD, as it's sometimes called) is the safest way to build up cardiovascular fitness. It's also the best type of exercise for burning fat, if you are trying to control your weight.

You'll read shortly about the Target Heart Rate, a very reliable way of measuring the intensity of your effort, no matter how in shape or out of shape you are. If you're just starting out, it's a good idea to stay toward the low end of your Target Heart Rate Zone.

Get in the habit of monitoring your heart rate often—during exercise (which is admittedly difficult if you're swimming), immediately after you stop, and then several minutes later. How high your heartbeat goes and how long it takes to return to normal will let you know if you're working too hard, not hard enough, or just right. See Chapter Four, "Before You Start," for more information.

MYTH #7—THE BEST WAY TO IMPROVE IS TO SWIM A LITTLE FARTHER EACH WEEK

This myth is the opposite side of the last one. Sure enough, long, slow distance training (LSD) and staying in your Target Heart Rate Zone is the safest, surest way to increase your cardiovascular fitness, which means increased endurance.

However, swimming endurance is only one aspect of a complicated sport. Technique plays a very important and often underestimated role in swimming, and LSD training is notorious for allowing sloppy habits to develop. Regular sessions concentrating on improving a swimmer's technique are very important for an all-around improvement in performance.

Technique can also be improved by regular sprint training, once the athlete is in good enough cardiovascular condition to handle the increased intensity. Sprinting also develops strength and *anaerobic* capacity, the ability to sustain intense efforts for longer periods.

So, while swimming farther is definitely good for you, remember that it's quality, not quantity, that really counts. Programmers have a favorite saying—"garbage in, garbage out," meaning that the information you get out of a computer is only as good as the information that went in. Beware of "garbage" mileage!

MYTH #8—WHEN YOU'RE IN GOOD SHAPE FOR SWIMMING, YOU'RE IN GOOD SHAPE FOR EVERYTHING

Sorry, it just ain't so. What swimming really gets you in shape for is *swimming*. It will also get you in pretty good shape for playing water polo or synchronized swimming. It's less of a help for bicycling or running, and when it comes to tennis or racquetball or, heaven forbid, mountain climbing, all that swimming won't do you much good at all.

There's a phenomenon known as *specificity* that's causing the problem. You can think of it as the opposite of generality. The more specific the adaptations your body's various systems make to the sport, the less they'll carry over to another sport.

We said earlier that swimming is mainly an upper-body sport. It's not going to do you much good for a lower-body sport like running. Sure, your heart and lungs are in great shape, getting lots of oxygen into your blood. But what good is that when there aren't enough blood vessels in your legs to deliver more blood down there, and your leg muscles don't have the necessary cellular machinery to process the oxygen?

Specificity even applies to different types of events in the same sport. If you train distance freestyle all the time, you can't expect your sprints to improve. Freestyle may help your butterfly quite a bit, because the movements are so similar, but it won't help your breaststroke much at all.

If you make a change in your training routine, such as bringing more sprinting into your workouts, take it easy for a while until your body can adjust. Likewise, if you take up another sport, be sure that you don't jump right into it with the same intensity you bring to your swimming workouts. Many injuries happen when people think they don't have to get into shape for a new sport; joints and tendons and muscles all have to go through a period of adaptation. This is especially a problem for swimmers who tend to have poor balance and loose joints. Take it easy!

MYTH #9—PRACTICE MAKES PERFECT

Masters coaches see it all the time. A newcomer shows up one day, filled with enthusiasm and hope and looking very promising. The swimmer comes regularly, getting into better and better shape, and then suddenly hits a plateau. "I need to swim more often," the swimmer thinks, and starts coming to more workouts. But to no avail. The swimmer tries swimming farther and longer each workout, but that doesn't seem to help. Swimming harder doesn't seem to be the answer, either. What went wrong?

When a swimmer hits a rut like this, when there's an honest attempt being made to keep improving by swimming farther, longer, or with higher intensity, you can be pretty sure that the problem is *technique*. While those millions of strokes, thousands of yards, and hours of practice have done wonders for improving the swimmer's cardiovascular system, they've done something quite different to the nervous system. Millions of strokes don't make the stroke get better. *They make it stay the same!*

Repetition is what trains the nervous system, developing

the neural pathways so that a movement becomes automatic. Think of a tennis player practicing serves, a golfer on the driving range, or a musician practicing scales. They aren't just batting at balls or mindlessly repeating a tune. They're asking themselves, "How was that one? What did I do right and what did I do wrong? How can I make the next one better?"

Don't continue along, blithely telling yourself that your stroke problems will "iron themselves out." They'll iron themselves *in*. It's not practice that makes perfect, it's the *practice of perfection*.

MYTH #10—SWIMMING HASN'T CHANGED MUCH OVER THE YEARS

On the contrary, swimming is one of the fastest changing sports there is, and if you haven't learned to swim in the last decade, you haven't learned to swim. Swimming used to be considered a survival skill, not a sport. And while many people know Captain Matthew Webb was the first swimmer to cross the English Channel (in 1875), few are aware that he swam *breaststroke* the whole way! The "over-arm" stroke was deemed inelegant and not a suitable stroke for true ladies and gentlemen.

Until the early 1950s, butterfly was considered an alternate way of swimming breaststroke, and until the late fifties, breaststrokers were also allowed to swim the entire race completely underwater. What a spectacle these races must have been, with some lanes containing butterfliers undulating across the surface while the breaststrokers glided silently along underwater in the lanes next to them. But the butterfliers became too fast, and the breaststrokers kept losing, and the rules were finally changed.

When the freestyle flip turn was developed, records fell aplenty, and when the rules were changed so the swimmers didn't have to swim up close enough to the wall to touch with their hands—the rulemakers decided that touching with the feet was sufficient—records fell once more. A similar thing happened when the backstroke flip turn was developed.

The biggest changes by far have occurred in the last two

decades as doctors, scientists, and technicians have brought ultra-high-speed movie cameras, kinesthetic analysis by computer, muscle biopsies, and even mass spectrometers into the natatorium.

One of the first casualties of this wave of high-tech research was the notion of the straight-armed, paddle-wheel stroke. Today's coaches are experts on such esoterica as hydrodynamic forces and Bernoulli's principle, and they're all proponents of something new—*the S-shaped pull*. In Chapter Three, we will discuss in detail all of these.

3
IT'S A MATTER OF STYLE

Floating along, breathing deeply, stroking rhythmically through the water—what a beautiful sport swimming is! A skillful swimmer can be as enjoyable to watch as a dancer or a gymnast, and swimming has more in common with these sports than you might think.

Because swimming is a timed competition like running or cycling, people often underestimate the crucial role that *technique* plays. Running is programmed into our genes and most of us learned cycling when we were kids by borrowing a friend's bike and sticking with it until we stopped falling down. Learning to swim, on the other hand, involves a much more complicated process. Because of this, many swimming books are devoted mainly to correct stroke techniques.

There's a fundamental problem with this approach, however. Psychologists have identified the right hemisphere of the brain as the dominant area in physical, nonverbal, spatially oriented activities such as swimming, while reading a book is definitely ruled by the left hemisphere.

Bogging down the verbal side of your brain with details may actually do more harm than good. One of Jackie Gleason's

A spectacular dive—racing style.

favorite tricks was to ask other golfers whether they inhaled or exhaled on the backswing. His poor victims would become so psyched out trying to analyze something they had always done unconsciously, their games would fall apart. The way to do something is to simply *do* it, much like Zen archers. Don't let thinking get in the way.

We're going to take a different approach, giving you basic guidelines on how swimming actually works and calling your attention to certain things to watch for as you swim. We'll also present a new approach to learning in general and give you some tips on how to use visualization (a right-hemisphere function) to improve your swimming.

The best way to actually learn the strokes is to *find an experienced teacher*. This could mean finding a friend, taking lessons at a private swim school, joining Red Cross, YMCA, or community school swimming classes, or finding a Masters coach who can set time aside to work on stroke instruction.

If you want to study frame-by-frame photos of each of the strokes, we recommend the excellent *Competitive Swimming Manual* by James "Doc" Counsilman and *Swimming Faster* by

Ernest W. Maglischo (see Bibliography). But be forewarned: these are highly technical books written primarily for other coaches. On a less technical level is *The Illustrated Swimmer* by Jan Prins, whose stick figures demonstrate major concepts often more clearly than underwater photographs.

A NEW (OLD) APPROACH TO LEARNING

Like learning a language or a musical instrument, there are great advantages to learning to swim when you're young. Learning very complex skills becomes more difficult as we age. But you *can* teach an old dog new tricks.

We've been so indoctrinated with school that we forget there are other ways to learn besides teachers and books. Consider how much a child has learned before ever setting foot in a classroom. Let's see if we can't rediscover our own natural, instinctive learning processes.

If you watch children play and pay attention to how they learn new skills, you'll see that they *observe, imitate, rehearse,* and *experiment*. They don't say, "*Tell* me how to do such and such." They say, "*Show* me!" Imagination and visualization are key elements in this process. A young child watches a parent hammering a nail or ironing laundry and tries to imitate these actions. So what if a hammer and nail or iron and ironing board aren't available? Almost anything will do—or even nothing at all. They improvise.

Also watch the way children incorporate learning into their lives. They don't stop playing and sit down to learn, like throwing a switch. It's all the same thing—they're learning while playing and playing while learning.

Try to bring this attitude of imitation and imagination to your swimming. Watch other swimmers—especially the good ones—not just with your eyes and brain, but with your nerves, your emotions, and your imagination. How would you *feel* slicing through the water with such speed, grace, and power? When you swim, try to recreate the feeling you imagined. Learn the rhythm of butterfly this way, or the timing of breaststroke's kick and glide.

Very young children naturally learn this way, but as grown-ups we have to make a conscious effort to go back and rediscover this simplicity. It's not only the most effective way to learn to swim. It can be fun, too.

IMPROVING YOUR EFFICIENCY IN THE WATER

If someone said you could take thirty seconds off your best time for a 400-yard swim without having to exert yourself any harder, would you be interested?

Many people, especially athletes coming from other sports, think you have to keep swimming harder and increasing your distance to become a faster swimmer, forgetting there's another very important way to improve: you can become more efficient. Why does one car get twice as many miles per gallon as another? Efficiency—in the form of improved combustion, less weight, and better streamlining.

If this sounds hard to swallow, you don't realize what a difference good technique can make. The reason efficiency is so much more crucial in swimming than in other sports is because you are performing your sport in *water*.

Hydrodynamics, the S-Shaped Pull, and Drag

When you run or pedal a bicycle, you actually push the earth, but, since it's a lot bigger than you, you're the one who moves: action and reaction. But when you push against water, it just slips away. Imagine running on ice or coming around a bend on your bike and finding gravel, and then you have an idea of what's going on hydrodynamically when you swim.

Many of us were told to keep our elbows rigid and to pull straight under our bodies when we first learned the crawl or freestyle stroke—the "paddle-wheel" style of swimming. When pioneer James "Doc" Counsilman began filming Olympic champions such as Mark Spitz with ultra-high-speed underwater cameras, coaches were astonished to find that without exception, they all bent their elbows—some as much as ninety degrees—and their hands instinctively traced an S-shaped, zigzag motion through the water.

How could they all be doing it wrong and still be Olympic champions?

Of course, they weren't doing anything wrong—everyone

else was! The "paddle-wheel" style of swimming is very ineffi-
cient. If you push straight back, the water moves away from
your hand and you end up pushing water that's already moving
backward. That's like running up a down escalator.

In boating, paddle-wheels were replaced by the screw-type
propeller. A propeller's blades never push backward, but move
across the water. As soon as the water they press on begins
moving, they're pressing somewhere else. The world-class
swimmers were doing the same thing unconsciously—moving
their hands sideways, searching out still water.

This is an application of Bernoulli's principle, which explains why airplanes fly. Bernoulli's principle says that the
faster a fluid travels, the less pressure it can exert perpendic-
ular to its direction of motion. For example, if you put your
hand out of a car window and tip the front edge upward, the air
going over the top has farther to travel than the air on the
bottom. In order to arrive back at the right place at the right
time, this air has to travel faster. According to Bernoulli's
principle, this higher speed means decreased pressure on top
of your hand, and the pressure below forces your hand upward.

When a swimmer sweeps his or her angled hand through the
water, the same thing happens. Because of the hand's angle,
there is more pressure on the palm side and less on the back,
and the difference makes the hand tend to move *forward* just
like a boat propeller. If you watch an excellent swimmer and
compare where his or her hand enters and leaves the water to
a fixed point on a lane line, you can actually see the hand
coming out *ahead* of the place where it went in.

Moving the angled hand sideways to the water like this is
called *sculling*, or sometimes *blading*. Watch synchronized
swimmers underwater; they do this all the time. Although
they seem to just wave their hands back and forth, this
generates enough power to hold their legs completely out of
the water. In fact, if you can talk a synchro swimmer into
showing you how this is done, it can do wonders for your
swimming.

In each stroke in the freestyle or crawl, the hand sculls in
toward the body, then changes angle and sculls away, making
the S-shape we spoke of earlier. (See the figure on page 23.) If

Good swimmers have what is called "a feel for the water." Their strokes are efficient because, either intuitively or through hard work, they have developed a pull in which their hands push back against the water, following a pattern of most resistance, through what is termed "still" water.

In freestyle this feels rather as if you are pulling your body along over your hand which has grabbed a handful of immovable (still) water—as though the water were a rock—and actually, that's close to what is happening. This powerful stroke is shaped like an elongated S-pattern with a high, bent elbow. The recovery phase, in which the arm relaxes and is brought back to the starting position, then follows.

you watch a butterflier swim directly over you, you can see these two S-shapes create a "keyhole" above you, round at the top, narrowing near the swimmer's middle to lower chest, and then fanning out again as the hands move down toward the swimmer's sides.

The other important hydrodynamic principle to keep in mind, one that's easier to understand, is *drag*. If Bernoulli's principle explains the forces making you go forward, drag is what holds you back. The first energy your muscles burn goes to overcoming drag—anything left over can be used for propulsion. You can improve your efficiency by reducing drag, and doing so mainly means maintaining good body position.

At this point, you may be wondering about swimmers

shaving their bodies before a big competition. For a long time, swimmers and coaches believed it reduced drag, but research has shown that the effect is almost unmeasurable. And yet shaving does seem to make swimmers faster.

Why? Maybe it's all psychological. If an athlete believes something will make him or her faster, it probably will, whatever it is. But some experts theorize that removing the body hair—and several layers of dead skin cells along with it— makes the swimmer's skin much more sensitive to drag and pressure, and this increased sensitivity accounts for the faster times.

Body Position

The key to reducing drag is correct body position. For freestyle and backstroke, this simply amounts to keeping the body horizontal and in a straight line. Letting the legs or hips droop, or wagging from side to side, creates enormous amounts of resistance.

Breaststroke and butterfly present different problems because you have to move your body up and down in the water just to swim the strokes correctly. The trick lies in finding the right amount of up-and-down movement to develop full power without creating excess drag.

Many swimmers aren't aware how much their head position affects the rest of their body. Backstrokers who hold their heads too high will force their hips to sink; freestylers who twist their heads to one side as they breathe will make their hips swing to the other side. Watch how a good butterflier's head controls the undulations of his or her body, diving down each time as his or her hands enter the water.

The kick also helps maintain good body position but provides very little propulsion (except in breaststroke). It keeps the legs and hips from sinking and counterbalances side-to-side motions caused by the movements of the arms and head. We'll go into more on the kick in a moment.

THE SIX PHASES OF THE FREESTYLE STROKE

We'll use the freestyle, or "crawl" stroke, to illustrate these principles of drag and propulsion. While this won't be a detailed analysis of the stroke, it will get you off on the right foot as you work on perfecting your own technique.

We'll divide the stroke into six phases and look at each of them separately:

- *The Entry,* when the hand enters the water in front of the head, beginning the new stroke

- *The Catch,* when the hand first applies pressure to the water

- *The Pull,* when the hand accelerates inward and the elbow bends, the upper curve of the S-shaped pull

- *The Push,* when the elbow begins to straighten and the hand pushes down toward the feet, the lower curve of the S-shape

Notice this swimmer's natural, relaxed, streamlined stroke. He's looking about 45 degrees from the water level, and his left hand has entered at a point where it can begin to accelerate inward to form the upper curve of the S-shaped pull.

- *The Release,* when the hand relaxes and prepares to exit by letting go of the water

- *The Recovery,* when the hand and arm come forward, preparing for the entry and the next cycle

Breaking such a graceful and fluid motion as freestyle into these six phases has to be a bit arbitrary; other people might do it differently. We find this way the most convenient for discussing the roles that drag and propulsion play in the stroke.

The Entry

In many ways, the entry is the most important part of your stroke; you can't stroke correctly unless your hand begins in the right position. Your goal on the entry should be to get your hand to the correct starting point while creating minimum water resistance. Because this is the only time you actually press your hand forward *against* your direction of travel, water resistance is extremely important.

If you watch a dozen swimmers, you will probably see a dozen different entries. This doesn't mean that any old entry will do, but that each of us has to find the one that works best for our own individual style.

Your hand should enter fingertips first, with your elbow held high so that the arm can follow your fingertips in through the same hole. This point should not be directly in line with your centerline, but off to the side. *Overreaching,* making the entry too near your centerline or even across it, is a serious stroke defect that causes your hips to fishtail through the water and strains the tendons in your shoulder. Check this by watching the bubbles that follow your hand—if they hit you smack in the face, you're reaching too far. Reach out in front more, instead of across, so they glance past your ear.

The hole your hand and arm enter through should be about *half* an arm's length in front of you, not at full extension. If you straighten your arm before it enters the water, you'll create more drag and tire the deltoid muscles at the top of your shoulder.

A common mistake, especially among male swimmers, is bringing the arm down forcefully, as if trying to start the next stroke with lots of momentum. Attacking the water like this sucks down large amounts of air bubbles which reduce your hand's "grip" on the water, the way gravel makes tires spin on pavement. When you look forward to watch your hands, you should see very few bubbles trailing them. (See also the next section on the catch.)

This can be solved by *slipping* your hand into the water instead of slapping your arm down. If your recovery is high and relaxed, it's a simple matter of letting the weight of the arm follow the fingertips into the water. Think of a diver's body slipping into the hole started by his or her hands, or imagine you're sliding your arm into a coat sleeve—let your arm follow your hand right through the hole.

The opposite problem is an entry that is *overcontrolled*. This is more common in female swimmers. The arm extends straight out over the water and almost stops as the swimmer places it gently in the water. This requires a lot of energy from the shoulder muscles, energy that should be saved for propulsion. The reason highly skilled swimmers look so relaxed and effortless in the water is that they don't waste energy where it isn't needed.

If you are guilty of overcontrolling your entry, the solution to the problem is much the same. Imagine that you are slipping your hand into a coat sleeve, but *relax* as you do it. Let gravity pull the weight of your arm into the water—you don't have to help at all. Bring that arm around and drop it. Aim and let go.

Experts disagree on the hand's angle from side to side. Some like the hand angled thumb down, others prefer little finger down, and a few prefer the hand to enter straight in. Each way had advantages and disadvantages, and there have been champions from all three styles. The important thing is to relax, trap as little air as possible, and get the hand in the right position for the rest of the stroke.

The Catch

The transition between the entry and the beginning of the

stroke is called the *catch*. Although it's a moment with no clear beginning or end, it's very important.

Remember we said water slips away from you when you press on it? Imagine you're walking on ice or biking through fine gravel. You don't just take a big step or press down hard on the pedals; you apply pressure gently, constantly testing, alert for the slightest signs of slipping.

Begin your stroke the same way. You can't muscle your way through water; it slips away. Begin gently, feeling the pressure, and then build up your hand speed. Doc Counsilman has found that champion swimmers' hands travel almost five times as fast at the end of each stroke as at the beginning. That's acceleration!

Once your hand enters the water, let your arm continue downward. There's no point in starting your pull close to the surface. Underwater photographs have shown that the champion swimmers usually begin applying pressure between twelve and eighteen inches below the surface. Press downward and outward, beginning the S-shaped pull. Try to actually feel the pressure beginning out at the ends of your fingers and building as it travels up your hand and along the inside of your forearm. Really feel it!

The Pull

Now we begin the first power phase of the stroke—the *pull*. As you press down and out, feeling pressure building from your fingertips up your hand and along the inside of your forearm, accelerate your arm. Keep accelerating as you "blade" your hand, turning in toward your centerline and beginning to bend your elbow. Be careful not to pull your hand in toward your stomach, though. If your hand drives water against your skin, you'll increase your friction against the water, slowing you down. Scull in toward an imaginary centerline below you.

Underwater photographs show champion swimmers reaching a maximum elbow bend between 90–105 degrees at a point near the middle or lower chest. However, it won't *feel* like it's bending that much. When Counsilman asked Olympic Gold Medalist Mark Spitz how much he bent his elbows, Spitz told him he didn't bend them at all. Counsilman's photos clearly showed his elbows bending in this 90–105-degree range, even though Spitz wasn't aware of it!

So if you feel as if you are bending your elbows ninety degrees, you may very well be bending them too much. Think instead about accelerating your hand down and through, and you'll probably be in the right range.

The Push

Obviously, our hands can't continue in a circle like a boat propeller. Past a certain point, there's nowhere else to go but back out. If the main motion of the pull phase was "out, down, and in," the main motion of the *push* phase is "back and to the side." The hand changes angle, blading in the opposite direction, and the arm presses back, straightening the elbow and continuing to accelerate.

Many beginning swimmers fail to push back all the way, a costly mistake. Because the hand travels at maximum speed through this part of the stroke, it's developing maximum propulsion.

One way to be sure you push back all the way is to touch your thigh with your thumb before releasing the water. If you touch your hip, feeling nylon instead of skin, you haven't pushed far enough. Coaches used to tell swimmers they should touch an inch or two below the bottom seam on their suit—before suits were so high cut!

The Release

As the catch was the transition between a relaxed entry and the application of power, *release* is the transition from power back to relaxation. When the hand can't push the water back any farther, it's time to let go. If the shoulder, arm and hand are tense at this point, the entire recovery motion—the main resting period between muscle contractions—will be tense.

Swimming teachers sometimes tell their students to push through until they actually fling the hand right up out of the water. While this helps a person push all the way back, the last bit that pops the hand out of the water wastes energy and drives the hips down into the water, spoiling the swimmer's body position and creating drag. The arm should relax *before* it clears the water.

As you finish the push, let your hand turn to its natural position, with the palm at your side facing your leg. This "knife" position lets it lift cleanly out of the water.

The Recovery

This sixth and final phase has a particularly appropriate name, because you "recover" the arm back to the starting position while your muscles rest and "recover" from the last burst of power and acceleration.

The secret to having a smooth, fluid stroke that looks effortless and feels as if you could go on forever is to relax, relax, *relax* on the recovery.

Here's a trick for developing smooth, relaxed recovery: think of bringing just your *elbow* around rather than your entire arm. Being concerned about your hand can cause the "overcontrolled" entry we mentioned earlier.

Bring your elbow high out of the water and around to the front—your hand has to come along too. You should now find your fingers in just the right spot to enter the water for the next stroke, as if by magic. Relax and drop your hands or fingers in.

This can prevent the two most common recovery problems: bringing the arm around with the elbow straight and the hand high in the air, and a recovery that's too wide and flat. Either of these tire the shoulders, and they both create drag by spoiling the body position. Bringing the hand too high causes an up-and-down bobbing motion, while a wide recovery causes fishtailing from side to side.

While lots of stroke drills have been developed to get the elbow high and keep the hand near the water, simply thinking about bringing your elbow around and relaxing everything else may be all you need.

FREESTYLE KICKING

In the "flutter" kick, the legs kick up and down alternately. The knees bend slightly as the feet kick downward, but, like

Notice how relaxed this swimmer's ankles remain as he kicks. The knees bend slightly; remember that your main propulsion comes from your upper body. Think of using your flutter kick to maintain your balance.

the elbows in the pull phase, this bending isn't usually noticed by the swimmer.

You may hear about two-beat kicks vs. six-beat kicks, broken rhythms, and so on. This is mainly a theoretical discussion, because most coaches let swimmers develop whatever kicking pattern comes naturally. As we've said before, the kick supplies a limited amount of propulsion in a good swimmer. While some swimmers kick three times on each arm stroke and others only once, they're all accomplishing the same thing: reducing drag by maintaining good body position. Legs and hips want to sink, and each armstroke creates off-center forces which tend to throw the body out of alignment. Kicking keeps the legs up and creates a counterbalancing force to prevent fishtailing.

If you rely on your kick for much of your forward speed, that's a sign your stroke has serious problems. On the other hand, if it takes you forever to kick to the other end of the pool, you probably lack flexibility in your ankles and feet; the foot has to bend a certain amount before Bernoulli's principle can work. Sometimes a person comes along with ankles so tight, he or she actually goes backward! You can increase your ankle flexibility by stretching and wearing fins. Your fins' extra resistance against the water will gently stretch your ankles and gradually increase their range of motion.

FREESTYLE HEAD POSITION

We've already mentioned the ways faulty entries, recoveries, and kicking can spoil the body's straight, streamlined position. Now let's look at the head.

Some swimmers move their heads around as if it will help their arms. Wiggling your head from side to side makes your shoulders, hips, and legs wiggle along behind you and causes a high increase in your drag. So keep your head movements to a minimum.

How high or low you carry your head also affects the way your body rides through the water. While there are many individual differences, a few general rules can help you find the head position that works best for you. First of all, find the part of your head that cuts through the water. If it's the very top of your head, your head is too low and you're looking too far down. On the other hand, if the water hits around your eyebrows, your head is too high and you're looking straight ahead too much.

What's the correct range? If we imagine a still-water level, your head and this waterline should meet about an inch-and-a-half to three-and-a-half inches above your eyebrows. To put it another way, you should be looking down at about 45 degrees from the water level, or slightly lower.

Despite the influence of many factors—buoyancy, kicking power, minor stroke differences, to mention just a few—it seems that swimmers generally hold their heads higher the faster they swim and sprinters on the whole tend to hold their heads higher than distance swimmers.

FREESTYLE BODY ROLL

Body roll is important for several reasons. Arm recovery is made easier because you lift your elbow more to the side than to the rear, and the rolling-back motion helps place the hand on entry. You don't have to twist your head as much to breathe, either. Just let it roll with your shoulders.

If you look at the second underwater photograph of the woman swimming freestyle on page 34, you'll notice that her shoulders are turned more than 45 degrees from horizontal. See how her rolling motion flows from the pulling and pushing motion of her left hand in the last three photos. Everything works together—the rolling makes the arms more efficient, and the arms produce the rolling motion.

Although it's possible to roll too much, the opposite problem is much more common. Relax and let your body roll as much as it wants. See if it doesn't make your recovery more relaxed and allow you to breathe more easily. You may also become more aware of your hand acceleration as your body rolls in reaction to your increased power.

About the only time rolling *too* much occurs is when there's a breathing problem. This can usually be corrected by exhaling sooner.

The swimmer's hand has just completed the entry and is beginning the catch phase, when she begins to "feel" the water. Notice how few bubbles are trailing behind her hand, a sign of a good entry, and how "high" her elbow is. Her hand is ready to begin pressing down and slightly out, forming the upper curve of the S-shaped stroke.

In the second photograph, we can see several important features of a good freestyle stroke. First of all, notice how high her elbow is, as if she were reaching over a barrel. You can also see that her shoulders have rotated quite a bit, bringing the larger muscles in her back into play, rather than just her arm and shoulder muscles. Good shoulder rotation also helps make the opposite arm's recovery easier. You can almost feel the way her hand is beginning to accelerate at this point.

In the third picture, the swimmer is nearing the end of the pull phase of her stroke. Notice how her elbow bend is approaching 90 degrees. (Remember it probably will not feel like you're bending your elbow that much when you're doing it correctly!) This is near the narrowest part of the S-curve, and in just a moment, her hand will press "back and out" in the push phase. Also note how her other hand is already entering the water, before her elbow, and how her shoulders are rotating back toward level.

Now the hand we have been following has almost reached maximum speed at the end of the push, straightening her elbow. Notice that her hand is still pressing back, however, not up. Her other hand has entered, trailing very few bubbles behind it. In a moment, her hand will relax, releasing the water, so that it can be pulled out, little finger first, on the recovery. This swimmer has a very narrow entry—perhaps too narrow—coming in almost to her centerline, but otherwise it is a very nice-looking stroke. Go back and look at this series of four once more, concentrating just on her shoulders to get a feeling of rotation.

FREESTYLE BREATHING

Look at the last photo on page 37, and you'll notice that the swimmer's mouth is in a trough created by his head moving forward through the water, as a boat creates a bow wave and a trough. It's located to the side and slightly toward your shoulder. Don't twist your head so far back that you cause your body to swing to the side. It's just a comfortable turn to the side, and your mouth should just barely clear the water.

Naturally, you should expect to feel out of breath when you're getting into shape, but some people find this feeling continues. If you've been swimming regularly for several weeks and you still find yourself gasping for air at the end of the pool, you may have a breathing problem. Though you may feel as if you aren't getting enough breath, it's usually caused by not *exhaling* completely. How can you fill your lungs if they aren't empty?

The cure is exhaling sooner, on the stroke *before* the one on which you will breathe. Don't wait until you're already lifting your head. When you breathe properly, it feels as if you have plenty of time for each breath. Many swimmers exhale gradually through the complete arm cycle, emptying their lungs completely so they're ready to be filled on the next breath.

Another common problem is breathing early, rushing the breath and lifting the head out of the water as shown in the photograph. (See "Early Breath" photos.) This "early" breathing makes your hips sink in the water, and can cause shoulder and neck pain. Fortunately, it's easy to fix. Just watch your hands and make sure that the hand on the opposite side has entered the water before you turn your head. For instance, if your breath will be to your left, make sure your right hand has entered the water first. Imagine your head *rotating* on an axis that runs up from your neck and out the top of your head— don't *lift* it.

The opposite problem—the "late" breath—occurs less often. A late breather sneaks a quick breath just before the arm comes down, resulting in an uneven, choppy stroke rhythm, a side-to-side fishtailing motion, with very little time to breathe. If you can already see your arm coming around at the instant your head comes up, you are breathing too late. (It's normal to

This swimmer is breathing too early. In order to be able to breathe while his opposite arm is still in the recovery phase, he has had to raise his head and shoulders out of the water. This requires a lot of energy, and makes his hips sink, creating more drag. The cure for this problem is to watch for the opposite hand entering the water in front of you before you breathe, and keep the lower eye in the water throughout the inhalation.

37

see it coming around *during* your breath, though.) The cure for this is to turn your head as your body rolls to that side. The head and shoulders should work together, not separately.

We also want to call your attention to a technique called *alternate* or *bilateral breathing*. Most of us have a side we prefer to breath on and experts disagree about whether a person who already breathes to one side should change. On the other hand, it can help smoothe out an unbalanced, asymmetrical stroke. It's nice in competition because you can see swimmers on either side and it's *very* helpful in open water. If you become an open-water addict, consider it. See Chapter Nine for more information.

THE OTHER THREE COMPETITIVE STROKES

As we said at the beginning of this chapter, we don't intend teaching you how to swim the strokes. But we do want to show you the basic principles at work behind the scenes so that you can work on technique on your own.

Backstroke

The backstroke has so much in common with freestyle that it used to be called the "back crawl." Many of the same principles apply—only upside down!

If you imagine a bar running in a straight line up from your neck, the place it would come out of the top of your head is approximately where your "waterline" should be. You should be looking up at about a 45-degree angle. Lifting your head higher will make you sink, and lowering it will decrease the effectiveness of your kick.

While there are many different rhythms for freestyle kicking, *all* good backstrokers use a six-beat kick, three kicks for each single arm stroke. The stroke causes much stronger side-to-side forces that have to be neutralized by a powerful kick.

Many beginners lie flat on their backs and sweep their arms to the side in a wide semicircle. Do you see the similarity between this and the paddle-wheel stroke? How can you do an S-shaped pull on your back?

The secret is body roll, and lots of it. If you rotate almost onto your side, you can perform the bent-elbow, S-shaped pull you did in freestyle. Your hand has to go extra deep on the *entry*, and the *catch* presses down and under as the pressure travels up your fingertips, hand, and forearm. The *pull* comes up toward the surface, with the elbow bending at the same 90–105-degree angle. If you're almost on your side instead of flat on your back, there's plenty of room.

Then *push* your hand down toward your side, causing your body to begin to roll to the other side. At the finish of the push, you flip your hand down so that your little finger comes out first when you *release* the water and begin your *recovery*. The recovery should be made with your elbow perfectly straight. Bringing your arm straight up over your shoulder

A racing backstroke start.

(like a paddle-wheeler) will help you place your next entry in line with your shoulder, where it belongs. Overreaching on backstroke entry causes even worse problems than it does in freestyle, and you can't check to see where your hand is going in. Keep the arm straight and bring it around in a vertical plane.

Many people begin to worry when they're getting close to the end of the pool. But if you turn around to look, you ruin your body position. That's what those used-car lot flags are for: they should be exactly five yards (or five meters in a long-course pool) from the end. Practice counting and you'll know how many strokes you take from the flags to the end of the pool. If you wonder when the flags are going to appear, count your strokes all the way from one end to the other. Many world-class swimmers count their strokes every length.

People often assume breathing won't be a problem in backstroke because their faces are out of the water. They wind up taking short little panting gasps instead of real breaths. Most experts recommend you inhale on one arm stroke and exhale on the other.

Butterfly

If you think of backstroke as freestyle upside down, you can call butterfly freestyle with both sides moving simultaneously. This ignores a lot of major differences between the two, but it does point out the fact that the S-shaped pull is almost identical in the two strokes. The only difference is that the body rolls from side to side in freestyle and stays flat in the fly.

This is what makes butterfly so strenuous to swim. Since you can't roll your body, breathing and the arm recovery become more difficult. Each stroke and kick combination has to help drive the shoulders up out of the water high enough for the next recovery, causing the undulating motion that makes butterfly so exciting to watch.

Here are some tips for better butterfly. Don't breathe on every arm cycle. Yes, it feels as though your lungs may burst, but raising your head out of the water every cycle will make your hips sink deeper and deeper and your swimming will become even *more* difficult as your drag increases. When you do breathe, raise your head as little as possible—try keeping your chin in the water. Also concentrate on diving back *down* after each breath, like a dolphin. This will help keep your hips up.

Butterfly gives you an excellent opportunity to see if you are really doing an S-shaped pull and bending your elbows. Your hands should almost touch in the center of the S-shaped pull at the transition between pull and push. While it helps to bend your elbow on freestyle recovery, keep your arms only slightly bent on the butterfly recovery.

Here's another tip: be sure to *glide* into your catch and get the feel of the water before you start your arm pull. Exaggerating this glide has helped many swimmers discover the stroke's difficult timing. It's also the only chance you get to rest!

One last thing. Wearing fins can also help you get the hang of timing, breathing, and undulating because they give you a little extra power. There's a danger, though: people sometimes become dependent on them. So don't abuse fins. The idea is to learn better butterfly *without* them.

Breaststroke

While breaststroke and butterfly have much in common with freestyle, breaststroke is very different. If it resembles any of the strokes, it must be butterfly. (Actually, it's the other way around—butterly resembles breaststroke, the stroke it evolved from.)

While it's hard to pick the most important differences, they basically come down to three: the stroke, the kick, and the timing. The underwater arm recovery isn't all that difficult to learn, but learning the kick and the timing can drive people to distraction.

First of all, since you must push your arms forward for the recovery *underwater* in the breaststroke, you have an unequaled opportunity to create *drag*. Through years of trial and error (not to mention changes in the rules for competition), the stroke has evolved in such a way that breaststrokers nowadays do only the first half of the S-shaped pull. Your hands should not pull down past midchest. Where a butterflier would begin the push phase after the elbows reach their maximum bend under his or her chest, the breaststroker just continues his or her hands around in a circle, shooting them back up to the front. No entry, no push, and no release. Just catch, pull, recovery.

Like the butterfly, there's a brief glide at the beginning of the catch when the arms are out in front. Exaggerating this glide can help you find the rhythm. As you get the hang of it, shorten the glide. In a sprint, the glide almost disappears—the hands slow just enough to catch for the next stroke.

The other problem, of course, is the kick. Breaststroke kick is probably the most difficult stroke technique to teach, and only a few people pick it up quickly. We could spend a whole chapter on it, and it still wouldn't help as much as having someone show you in the water.

We will give you one very valuable clue, though. Remember when we talked about Bernoulli's principle, and said it is the difference in pressure between the top and bottom sides of your hand or foot that creates propulsion? Breaststroke kick is the only one where the *high* pressure is developed on the *bottom* of your foot—in all the other kicks, the high pressure is on the top. No wonder it feels different! Try to feel the pressure on the soles of your feet and you may learn the kick more easily.

THE MOST SERIOUS OF ALL STROKE DEFECTS

As we've dissected the four competitive strokes, we've mentioned several of the problems swimmers can develop, and ways to overcome them. However, there is one stroke defect that deserves to have its own section—the *dropped elbow*.

Look once more at the underwater photographs of the woman freestyler on pages 34 and 35. In the first one, just after her entry, you'll see that her elbow is higher than her hand. In the next photo, this is even more pronounced, and her arm is arched as if she were reaching over a barrel. Although it's harder to see, her hand is probably still preceding her elbow in the third picture.

A dropped elbow is the most serious stroke defect a swimmer can have. While the woman in the freestyle series is

This photograph illustrates several features of a perfect recovery. Notice first that the elbow is higher than the hand—remember to think of relaxing your hand and letting your elbow bring it around. You can see how relaxed the swimmer's hand is. Also note how he has turned his head just enough to breathe in the "pocket" formed by his motion through the water, without angling his head back toward his shoulder or lifting it out of the water.

getting pull and lift from her fingertips, forearm, and even parts of her upper arm, a swimmer with a dropped elbow is only pulling with the palm.

Not only is the surface area of your arm nearly three times greater than that of your hand; but take a close look at your forearm. Do you see how it bears a distinct resemblance to an airplane wing—flat on the underside, arched across the top? We mentioned that Bernoulli's principle explains how boats can be propelled the way airplanes fly. Your forearm, *if held at the correct angle*, makes an ideal surface for creating propulsion during the inward sculling motion of the S-shaped pull.

Here is our favorite drill for developing a high elbow pull: Imagine that you are swimming in a lake that's filled with submerged logs. They're soggy and rotten and you don't want to touch them any more than you have to, so you reach *over* each one as you swim, touch its far side with your palm, and *push* it under you. If you arch your elbow high enough over it, the disgusting stuff won't get on your arms, but if you drop your elbow, look out!

4
BEFORE YOU START: SOME GENERAL PRINCIPLES

In 1968 a small paperback book appeared that sparked a revolution that is still going on today. Not only did Dr. Kenneth Cooper's book become an enormous bestseller, but the book's title became a popular new word—*Aerobics*.

Derived from a root word for "air," aerobics refers to any type of exercise in which the muscles don't consume oxygen faster than the heart and lungs can replenish it. In other words, it's *cardiovascular* exercise, using the heart and lungs.

Cooper's book emphasized the long-term health benefits offered by aerobic exercise: reduced blood pressure, decreased heart attack risk, enhanced self-esteem, better weight control, and the list goes on. These may also be your main reasons for becoming an adult fitness swimmer.

This chapter will be devoted to giving you a deeper understanding of how exercise affects your body so you'll have a better understanding of how to reach your fitness and performance goals.

ADAPTATION

Have you ever had a job where you had to stand on your feet all day? Remember thinking that you'd be crippled for life after the first few days? And then, after a few weeks, your body got "used to it." You can think of many similar examples—lifting heavy things, getting up at a different hour, living in a different climate. In each of these cases, your body has changed itself—*adapted*—to the new demands being placed on it.

Adaptation is the fundamental concept of all athletic training. Another common term for this "adaptation/getting-used-to" phenomenon, when it's applied to sports, is "getting in shape." If you've been swimming for a few months, you are probably amused to remember how often you had to stop and catch your breath when you were first starting out. That's because you've adapted to swimming. You're in "better shape" now.

STRESS AND RECOVERY

Adaptation has two components: *stress* and *recovery*. The *stress* is the time when we are asking our bodies to do something difficult—the work phase. *Recovery* is the interval between stresses when our bodies get a chance to heal from the last stress and prepare for the next one. In other words, rest.

The secret is balancing the two periods. Too much stress and our bodies won't be able to adapt. We'll get sick or hurt ourselves. Too little stress and our bodies won't feel any need to adapt. There also has to be enough—but not too much—recovery.

For a simple example, let's look at suntanning, your body's attempt to adapt to the stress of the sun's harmful radiation. If you go out in the sun for only five minutes, your body won't feel much of a need to adapt—too little stress. But if you go out for six hours your first day, you'll burn badly—too much stress. The right amount would be in between.

You might decide, "An hour's worth of sun is the right amount. I'll go out for one hour the first Saturday of each month." Obviously, you won't get a tan that way, either. The recovery time between the stresses is too great. What happens if you go out for one hour every other hour? You burn again—too little recovery time between the stresses.

GETTING IN SHAPE

This is what athletic training is all about: balancing the periods of stress with the periods of recovery in just the right amounts.

Several authorities have picked twenty minutes of exercise, three days a week as the "magic number" for the minimum amount of aerobic exercise that people need—i.e., the minimum amount of stress needed to cause cardiovascular adaptation.

But different types of training require different mixtures of stress and recovery. For instance, three days a week is the recommended *maximum* for serious weight training. That's because lifting weights to the point of exhaustion (that's what we mean by *serious*) is a *big* stress that needs longer recoveries. And while the minimum of twenty minutes a day, three days a week is good for you, it provides only a minimum amount of adaptation.

HOW MUCH TRAINING?
LET YOUR HEART BE YOUR GUIDE

How do you know exactly what the right amount of training will be for you? How can you tell if you're training enough to reach your goals, but not so much that you're asking for trouble? There is only one person who can tell you—yourself.

Each of us comes with a very sensitive, built-in gauge that measures not only the stress we place on our bodies, but whether we're getting enough rest in between. It even tells us what kind of shape we're in. It's called the heart!

While swimming is mostly upper body exercise, and running and biking put more demands on your lower body, they *all* put demands on your heart. Stress, recovery, and adaptation apply to the heart just like any other part of your body. Here are a few of the things your heart can tell you:

During exercise: Comparing your pulse to the target heart rates mentioned later in this chapter will tell you if you're working too hard or not hard enough.

Immediately after exercise: Measuring how quickly your heart rate drops back down after exercising will tell you what kind of shape you're in overall. If your heart rate drops from your target rate to under 100 beats per minute in a minute or less, you're in excellent shape.

The next day: Another indicator of your condition is your heart rate when you first awaken in the morning, before getting out of bed. Generally, the lower the resting heart rate, the better shape you're in.

Throughout the swimming season: Following your resting heart rate over a long period of time will give you valuable feedback. If you take your pulse every morning before you get up, you'll find that it's usually within a few beats of the same figure. Then, if it's several beats per minute higher one morning (10 percent or more), that's a sign that you may not have recovered fully from your last workout. You might want to take it easy that day, or maybe even take the day off. You're in danger of overtraining!

TARGET HEART RATES

Your ideal heart rate for optimum aerobic training is usually calculated to be somewhere between 60–80 percent of your maximum heart rate. If you can keep your heart rate in this range for at least twenty minutes a day, three days a week, you'll measurably increase your level of aerobic fitness.

What is your maximum heart rate? An easy way to arrive at a figure is to subtract your age from 220. This will give you an approximate maximum heart rate. Then your Target Heart Rate will be between 60 and 80 percent of that. Let's use someone thirty-eight years old as an example:

Maximum heart rate $(220 - age) = 220 - 38 = 182$

60% of maximum heart rate $= .6 \times 182 = 109$
80% of maximum heart rate $= .8 \times 182 = 146$

So our thirty-eight-year-old will want to aim to maintain a heart rate between roughly 110 and 145 beats per minute during workout.

If all this math is confusing, or you haven't seen your calculator since last April 15, on page 49 is a chart of Target Heart Rates for people between twenty-five and seventy-five.

BEFORE YOU START: SOME GENERAL PRINCIPLES

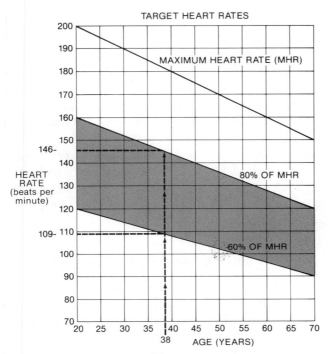

TARGET HEART RATES

Copyright © 1985—Katherine Vaz and Chip Zempel

To Find Your Target Heart Rate Zone: Locate your age along the bottom line. Go up until you hit the first 60 percent Maximum Heart Rate (MHR) line and then find the corresponding Heart Rate on the vertical axis on the left. This is the lower limit of your Target Heart Rate Zone (shaded area). Continue up from your age and find the heart rate corresponding to 80 percent MHR, the upper limit of your Target Heart Rate Zone. (The example shows finding the Target Heart Rate Zone for a 38-year-old swimmer, from 109 beats per minute to 146 beats per minute.) You can find your theoretical Maximum Heart Rate by continuing directly up from your age to the top line on the chart.

Here are some things to keep in mind about your THR Zone: If you are just starting out, stay near the lower limit of your THR Zone. Well-conditioned athletes training for maximum aerobic endurance should aim for the higher limit. As you will see in Chapter Six, there are time when you will exceed the upper limit in anaerobic training for lactic acid tolerance, and in sprint training, your heart rate will drop well below the lower limit during the rests between swims.

Find your age along the bottom line. Go up until you find the beginning of the shaded area. Read across to the left side of the chart and get the number of beats per minute. That's the lower limit of your Target Heart Rate Zone. Now continue upward from your age until you reach the top of your Target Heart Rate Zone, and read the upper limit off the left side of the chart. (We've used our thirty-eight-year-old as an example again.)

One of the nice things about using Target Heart Rates is that they aren't affected by your swimming skill, only by how hard you're working. You may actually be getting a better cardiovascular workout than that National Champion over there in the fast lane!

How to Use Your Heart Rate

The easiest place for most people to find a pulse is at the neck, between the Adam's apple and the big muscle at the side. Count your pulse for ten seconds and multiply by six to find out the number of beats per minute. Make sure that you take it as soon as you stop swimming—it can drop enough in fifteen or twenty seconds to give you a completely inaccurate idea of how hard you're working. (If your sixes multiplication table is kind of rusty and you don't want to bring your calculator out on the pool deck, take your pulse for six seconds and multiply by ten.)

We've already mentioned that you want to aim for your Target Heart Rate for the best aerobic training effect, but there are many times in a swimming workout when you might want to go above or below this number. Swimming isn't a totally aerobic sport.

For example, if you haven't been getting any aerobic exercise at all, it's a good idea to stay down at the very low end of your Target Heart Rate Zone for the first few weeks. If you have any serious medical conditions, you may not even want to get into the zone at all.

On the other hand, an athlete in excellent condition will want to reach up near the top of that zone and exceed it some of the time. Since the sprints and middle-distance races involve *an*aerobic energy, you have to go beyond your aerobic training levels to stress those energy systems and bring your heart rate up to higher pulse rates.

When a sprinter swims fifty yards as fast as he or she can in a meet, his or her heart rate is very low at the start (except for the effects of adrenalin) and he or she needs to be able to get it up very close to maximum heart rate in a very short period of time. In order to duplicate the stress of sprinting in workouts, sprinters will swim a short distance very hard and then take a long rest. The effect of this is that their heart rates are constantly shooting up above their Target Heart Rate Zones, and then dropping back down below them with each swim. We'll look at this in more detail in the next chapter.

GETTING STRONGER

Aerobic training and adaptation get us into better shape by increasing our endurance. But the heart and lungs are not the only muscles that need to adapt. The muscles that move us around also become stronger as stress and recovery force *them* to adapt.

What is the stress that strengthens our muscles? *Resistance.* This is the key not only behind weight training, but also in using fins, which make our legs push harder on the water; paddles, which do the same for our hands; and various other mysterious devices found lying around pool decks. Collectively, they're known as "training aids." Following is a quick rundown of the most common ones.

Training Aids

The days when all you needed was a body of water and some cutoff shorts are gone, and swimming has now become an equipment-laden, high-tech sport. Paddles, fins, kickboards, and pull-buoys litter the end of each lane, not to mention the more exotic items like tether systems and isokinetic swim benches. These devices help improve your swimming in several ways. They can increase your awareness of your technique, provide greater resistance in the water much like weight training, and allow you to isolate part of your swimming technique for concentrated practice.

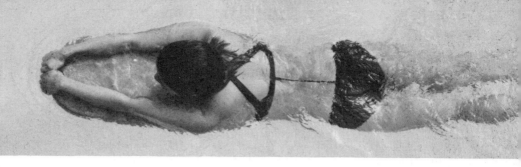

Kickboards can give the legs a concentrated workout.

The substantial increase in propulsion that *fins* provide makes them the only training aid that's popular in recreational swimming as well as "serious" swimming. They cause more resistance for the large muscles of your legs and their gentle pressure promotes greater ankle flexibility. Less skilled swimmers get more confidence, an appreciation of how it feels to go fast, and a better awareness of their body position when they wear fins. They can also help a slower swimmer keep up with a faster workout partner.

Fins with a flexible blade are more comfortable than the stiffer ones. Look for ones that won't rub against your ankle bones or the top of your heel. You may also want to pick a pair that floats if you plan on using them for body surfing or swimming in open water.

You can use fins for kicking with or without a kickboard, or wear them while you stroke. They can be especially helpful for getting the hang of butterfly's undulating motion. They really have only one drawback: some swimmers will become so used to the extra speed they get from wearing fins, that they never feel right without them. Coaches recommend that you use them for no more than 25–30 percent of your total yardage.

Kickboards make it easier to practice kicking by keeping your upper body afloat, and they also provide some resistance. The full-sized boards provide the most buoyancy and resistance, but some swimmers and coaches prefer to cut boards in half to achieve a more natural body position. Holding the board near the front with the arms extended is the most comfortable, while holding it farther back creates more resistance and makes the back and stomach muscles work harder to keep the body straight.

Unfortunately, kickboards change the body position and make it almost impossible for the body to roll, so your kick doesn't bear much resemblance to the kick you use when you're swimming. Holding your head up can cause neck strain after a while, and you may prefer to keep your face in the water. You'll also be less tempted to talk to the other swimmers and concentrate more on your own workout!

Because kicking doesn't provide much propulsive force, you don't need to kick more than about 20–25 percent of your workout. After your kicking, be sure to loosen your shoulders up well before starting any hard swimming. Be aware that hyperextension when holding the board may cause shoulder strain; try kicking *without* a board as well.

Paddles are worn on the hand and create more resistance for the arms and shoulders. (They're notorious for causing shoulder problems for this same reason.) Be sure to warm up well before using them. The larger sizes are preferred by the stronger swimmers and those without shoulder problems. You can use paddles alone when you swim normally, or combine

Kickboards allow you to isolate your leg muscles and develop a better sense of balance and propulsion.

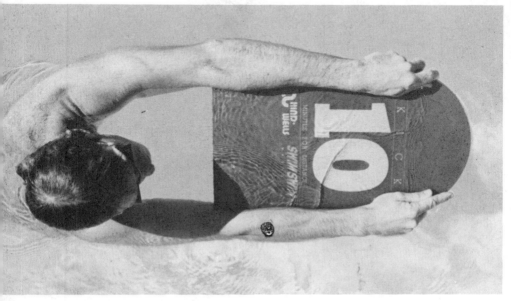

them with pull-buoys or other devices to concentrate on just your arm stroke.

Paddles also make you more aware of your hand movements. If they twist on your hand or pull away from your palm, you're doing something wrong at that point in your stoke. Dropping your elbows often causes this.

Pull-buoys are usually made of two cylinders of styrofoam held together by a strap, and you hold them between your

Vary your workouts and increase all-important upper-body strength by using pull-buoys.

Hand paddles come in a variety of shapes and sizes. Try using a pair to improve your follow-through and recovery!

thighs to support your hips. Because of this support, you can reduce your kick and concentrate on your pulling. Remember that most of your power comes from your arm stroke. Pull-buoys also create a small amount of drag resistance, slowing down most swimmers a little. They can be used with or without paddles.

Tubes, bands, and *rings* are all devices that attach to a swimmer's feet, preventing kicking entirely. Some provide buoyancy and their size (and how much they change the swimmer's body position) determines how much resistance they create. They're often used in combination with paddles and/or pull-buoys.

Most training aids cause some change in the swimmer's body position, which causes concern for the technique-oriented coach. Among the many things people have come up with to increase a swimmer's drag while maintaining correct form, perhaps the best is the *drag-suit.* Made of nylon tricot, it resembles a regular swimsuit with pockets that catch water and create resistance. The faster you swim, the more resis-

A drag-suit increases your resistance to the water, making your stroke-by-stroke efforts much more difficult.

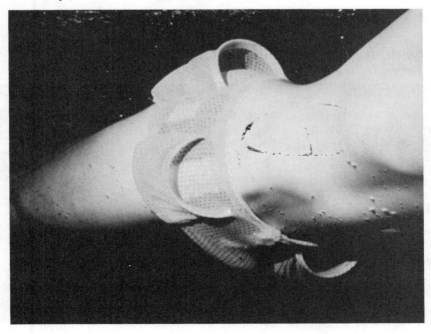

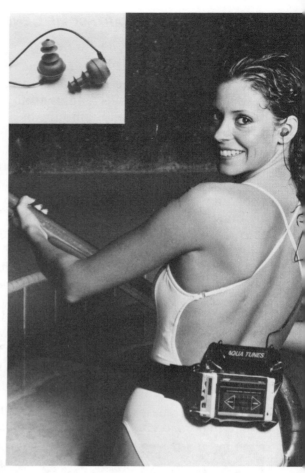

Glide along to Handel's Water Music with the small waterproof transistor radios now available.

A tether system allows a serious swimmer to put in a good workout in a small backyard pool.

Everybody into the pool! Fins can improve ankle flexibility and strengthen your legs.

tance it creates, making it beneficial for beginners and experts alike.

Since the resistance is near the center of your body instead of out at your hands or feet, and it doesn't affect your buoyancy, a drag-suit may be the ideal training aid. There are other ways of causing a similar effect, such as wearing pantyhose or wearing an old T-shirt or sweatshirt with the sleeves cut off.

Tether systems are a bit more specialized than the previous aids we've looked at. They create resistance by physically tying the swimmer to some object. This can be anything from a single rope tied around the swimmer's waist at one end and the starting block at the other, to an elastic piece of surgical tubing, or a complicated system of weights and pulleys lifted by a rope as the swimmer swims away from that end of the pool.

Tethers have several disadvantages. They're complicated to rig up, there can't be other swimmers in the lane when one is in use, and they can be very dangerous. If you use a tether that involves weights or elastic, ask yourself what will happen if something breaks. Swimmers and coaches have been injured by flying fittings, so be careful!

On the other hand, a tether system can be extremely challenging if it's set up so you can almost make it to the other end of the pool before the pull becomes too strong. And it's really the only way a strong swimmer can get a good workout in a small backyard pool.

These are only a sampling of the most common training aids. Some pools have underwater windows, where a coach can get a good look at your technique. The very best facilities may even have remote-control videotaping equipment. Special extra-long mirrors are made for placing on the bottom of a lane so you can watch your stroke as you swim over it. (You can get a somewhat similar effect by swimming in still water on a sunny day and watching your shadow.) There are even Walkman-like waterproof radios so your coach can talk to you while you're swimming.

There are lots of methods to help you train out of the water, too. Most of these take the form of stretching and weight lifting. "Dry-land training" is a very big part of any serious competitive swimming program, and we'll look at this aspect in Chapter Six.

The Pace Clock

The pace clock is an entirely different class from the more mundane training aids like pull-buoys and kickboards. As you'll see in the next chapter, swimming workouts are almost always divided into shorter swims on timed intervals. This is where the pace clock comes in.

Because we are interested in measuring minutes and seconds in swimming, a pace clock doesn't have an hour hand. The face is marked off with "60" at the top, "15" on the right, "30" at the bottom, and "45" on the left, making it easier to figure your time at a glance. If you left when the second hand was on the top and it's just passing "53" when you touch the wall, you know your swim took you fifty-three seconds (or 1:53, or 2:53, etc.).

A pace clock will help you keep track of your interval times. It's the most graphic way to test your improvement and progress.

The ideal way to budget your energy over a long distance is to swim at a steady pace, making all your intermediate *split* times the same—a process known as "even-splitting." In a 500-yard swim, for instance, each of your 100s would be one-fifth of the total time. With a little practice, you may become so good at reading a pace clock that you can glance up at it *during* a swim and figure out your "splits."

While there are digital models available, most people prefer a sweep second hand because you can keep track of your intervals graphically. For instance, if you were supposed to start each of your swims on an interval of 2:15 (two minutes and fifteen seconds), your intervals will almost march their way around the clock. First you leave on the top, then begin the next one on the right, then down, then to the left, progressing around the clock by quarters.

You can even use this knowledge to keep track of how many intervals you've swum. If you left on the top and your interval is 2:15, then the next time you leave on the top, it will be swim number five, then nine, thirteen, and so on, adding four each time around because you are repeating quarter minutes. It doesn't matter if your interval is 1:15 or 2:15 or 3:15, the seconds work out the same way. Likewise, if you are swimming every 1:20, starting on the top, the swims that start on the "60" would be the first, fourth, seventh, and tenth, adding three each time because twenty seconds is one-third of a minute.

Keeping track of how many intervals you've swum can be a real challenge in a long and difficult workout, especially when you're becoming tired. Here's another trick that will help keep track of how many repeats you've swum: use the little plastic disks on the lane line like beads on an abacus. Each time you do one of your swims, slide another one down. It's a neat trick—as long as you're sure the people in the lane next to you aren't using that lane line already, and you remember to slide one over each time.

One More Training Aid

If you decide that you really want to go beyond just being fit and get the sense of accomplishment that comes from making measurable progress and improvement, let us suggest one other very valuable training aid—a *workout book*. It can be as simple as a note in the bottom of each day's box on your calendar—"2,500 yds. A.M.—weights with Terry P.M."—or as complicated as a data base maintained on a home computer. The simple act of keeping a record of how often you work out can be a motivator in itself.

You can use it for a lot more, too. You could have a section where you write down your goals. You could keep track of your weight and how many calories you've been eating if weight control is one of your goals.

You could keep track of your favorite workouts, too. They can come in handy on those days when you have to train by yourself or when the coach asks you to write your own workout. You can keep a record of your resting heart rates and even your blood pressure if you have a home testing kit.

One of the best uses of a training log is to have a section where you keep track of your times—personal bests in workouts or in organized meets.

THE TWELVE-MINUTE TEST

This test for assessing a person's fitness level was first presented in Dr. Cooper's pioneering book, *Aerobics*. It consists of the athlete running as far as possible in twelve minutes, and comparing that distance to a chart that rates his or her fitness on a scale of one to five. Twelve minutes is the minimum time to give an accurate measurement of cardiovascular fitness—anything less than that relies too much on the *anaerobic* energy system we use for sprinting.

Since many of us would rather die than run for twelve minutes, other charts were developed for testing fitness levels by swimming and cycling. Unfortunately, the swimming table isn't nearly as accurate as the charts for running or cycling because swimming well depends so much on technique. An ex-Olympian who hasn't exercised in twenty years might still swim farther in twelve minutes than a fit, active person who just learned to swim at the "Y" last summer. It's the nature of the sport, so take these relative fitness levels with a grain, or better yet a rounded tablespoon, of salt.

Even though the twelve-minute swim may not tell as much as we'd like about our *absolute* fitness level, it's still excellent for measuring your own personal progress. If you do a twelve-minute swim every few months, you should see a very satisfying improvement. If you keep track of your resting heart rate, you can get an idea of how much of your improvement comes from increased fitness and how much from better technique.

Here are some pointers for your first twelve-minute swim. Remember what we said about pacing. If you swim too fast, you'll have to stop and give yourself a chance to catch your breath. Too slow and you'll suddenly discover that you have a lot of energy left over for a mad sprint is the last few lengths. Aim for "even splits."

If you do your twelve-minute swim and feel you could have

swum at a better pace, do another one in a few days. Try to determine your ideal time for each 100 yards and either watch the pace clock or have a friend signal whether you're holding your pace, going too fast, or slowing down.

It shouldn't take more than two or three tries to get a fairly reliable twelve-minute swim measurement. Remember, you aren't shooting for the *perfect* twelve-minute swim; you just want an idea of where you stand. Record the date and your distance in your workout book. Try it again in a few months. You'll be pleased to see how much you've improved.

WEIGHT CONTROL AND EXERCISE

The only way to achieve a long-term, healthy weight loss is through a combination of aerobic exercise and a reduction in the number of calories you take in. Diet alone won't do it.

Scientists have recently discovered a biological mechanism that they call the *set point* (your personal metabolic regulator). It acts a bit like the thermostat in your house, controlling how fuel is burned in your body. If you reduce your caloric intake and start losing weight, you quickly reach a plateau where it becomes much more difficult to lose any more. So you reduce your intake even farther, and you lose a few more pounds and level off again.

This is your set point at work, a mechanism that evolved to increase our chances of survival during famine periods. When you lowered your caloric intake below the minimum amount needed for the basic metabolic energy requirements for producing warmth, keeping your heart beating, replacing dead cells, and so on, your body assumed that starvation was imminent and automatically began to reduce the amount of fuel you burned by lowering your metabolism. You gave it less fuel, so it burned less.

There is a very simple way to get around this set point problem, though. All you have to do is exercise regularly. Exercise *raises* your metabolism, meaning that you burn *more* calories. After a thirty-minute exercise session, your body will continue to burn energy at a higher rate for *several hours* after you've stopped exercising, and your resting metabolism will tend to remain higher. You'll wind up burning even more fuel than you would expect to from thirty minutes of exercise.

The secret to losing weight, then, is to make your body burn more calories as well as trying to take in less fuel.

Another problem with merely dieting is that you could lose muscle as well as fat. Muscle is much harder to gain back, and if you don't exercise, all the weight that you do put on will be fat. If you lose muscle only to gain weight back as fat, you'll be weaker and even less active than you were before. As you can see, this can start a vicious cycle.

If you combine diet *and* exercise, though, you may lose several inches while not being able to notice a weight loss on the scale. Why? You are losing fat, which is very loose and bulky, while replacing it with firm, tight muscle. Muscle is much denser and takes up much less room pound for pound. Don't be too concerned with how many pounds you are losing or not losing. Instead, watch the tape measure and the thickness of the skin you can pinch.

The most efficient way for your body to burn fat is for you to exercise and consume complex carbohydrates and plenty of water. Without these two items, your body can't consume fat as efficiently and winds up producing waste products that can affect your health. This is why so many athletes eat carbohydrate-rich foods like pasta, potatoes, and bread, that were once thought to be forbidden without gaining weight. The carbohydrates they eat and the exercises they do burn the fat off their bodies very effectively.

How fast can you lose weight safely? A good rate of weight loss to aim for is 1–1.5 percent of your total body weight per week. That may not sound like much, but any faster than that and you risk losing muscle along with the fat, which you don't want to do. Remember that losing weight requires a change in lifestyle; hoping for a quick and easy solution to your weight problem is *no* solution.

The average person needs a minimum of 1,600–1,800 calories per day for basic energy requirements. This is the level below which the set point phenomenon begins to occur and you start to burn muscle as well as fat. For this reason, many experts recommend that you stay well above this figure and consume approximately 2,000 calories per day. You can expect to lose about two pounds a week if you reduce your daily caloric intake by 500 calories and swim for one hour each day. This conveniently puts most of us in that safe 1–1.5 percent per week weight-loss range.

Two pounds a week doesn't sound like much. You can remind yourself, though, that it's *all* fat that's being lost. And you're doing a lot to improve your mental and physical health at the same time. Remember—there's more to good health than just losing pounds!

5
WORKING OUT

Swimming back and forth becomes pretty boring after a while. You settle into a groove, your technique stops improving, and once your body adapts to the workload, your fitness stops increasing. Oh, no, you think, I'll have to keep swimming farther and farther if I want to get any better.

As we pointed out in Chapter Two, this doesn't have to be the case. If you want to really improve your swimming—and enjoy it more at the same time—you should quit the old back-and-forth and step up to the exciting world of real swimming workouts.

FROM LAPS TO WORKOUTS

You've decided to make the big step from lap swimming to *training*. Even though you've worn this suit, this cap, and these goggles for many months, you feel as self-conscious as you did the first day you stepped onto the pool deck.

You walk over to the only person with street clothes on. "Are you the coach?" He tells you to find a lane about the right speed and says, "The warm-up's on the board."

Swimming is an excellent exercise for pregnant women.

You look where he pointed. The chalkboard looks like this:

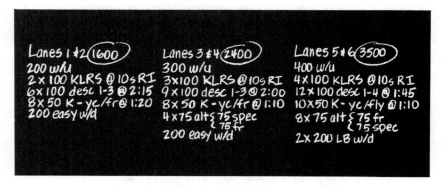

w/u = warm-up
KLRS = kick/left arm only/right arm only/swim
10sRI = 10-second rest interval
desc = descend
yc/fr = your choice/freestyle

w/d = warm-down
spec = your specialty stroke
K = kick
alt = alternating
LB = lung buster

Welcome to the world of swimming workouts! Like traveling in another country, raising children, or changing careers, it's a world unto itself. Someone's changed all the rules, the landmarks are different, and everyone talks funny.

Our goal in this chapter is to help you through your period of culture shock and turn you into a seasoned pro.

GETTING ORGANIZED

One of the key differences between most lap swimming programs and workout programs is organization. The ideal workout is structured to give the most people the maximum benefit in the least amount of time. A lot of newcomers experience difficulty and confusion because they do not know all the etiquette and jargon.

Etiquette

Etiquette keeps organized workouts *organized*. Rules for behavior keep workouts running like well-oiled machinery and help people function on a polite, cooperative, and social level. Let's face it. The more intense a situation is, the more important etiquette becomes—and swimming workouts can be pretty intense at times!

The Golden Rule

If swimming etiquette can be summed up into one single rule, it would be this:

Don't interfere with the other person's workout.

Most swimming etiquette comes down to staying out of the way of other swimmers, quite a tall order in a pool filled with thirty, forty, or more swimmers, ranging from beginners to seasoned competitors. But it can be done. Here's how:

Which lane to use? The coaches (or the swimmers, if the coaches aren't paying enough attention) will try to group swimmers of the same speed together, and most workouts have fast lanes, medium lanes, and slow lanes.

This is such an obvious place to begin organizing a workout that it might seem trivial, except there are always people who walk up to the pool and just jump into whatever lane seems the least crowded. Then they get angry at the impatient person who just ran them over.

You may be shuffled around for the first few workouts until you and the coach find just the right spot. Once you've found your lane, you'll swim there most of the time. But don't become a stick-in-the-mud—there are lots of reasons why you might get moved temporarily or permanently.

People with a streak of competitiveness look at the next faster lane as a goal to shoot for, and getting "moved up" is for many a bigger deal than a promotion at work.

On the other hand, if you stay away from the water for a while, you may get moved down a lane because you can't keep up with your lane partners anymore.

Think of your lane assignment as your lane *assignment*, not *your lane*. (As in, "What are you doing in *my* lane? That's *your* lane over there!")

Traffic patterns: The moment you have more than one person in a lane there's a chance of head-on collisions. Swimming etiquette has developed a very simple way of dealing with this: *circle swimming.* Just like on a highway, you keep to your right. The stripe on the bottom of the pool is like the dotted line down the middle of the road. When you get to the other end of the pool, you turn and come back on the other side. Simple, isn't it?

There is one major variation on this, called *lane splitting,* and it only works when there are two (and only two) people in the lane. Each of you takes one half of the lane, as divided by the stripe on the bottom. You go down and come back *on the same side* of the lane. Some coaches and clubs don't like this— every once in a while, someone forgets he or she isn't circling, and comes back on the wrong side—so be sure that it's allowed. Of course, if a third person comes into your lane, you have to go back to circling.

You may run into slight variations—circling in two lanes, where you go down one lane and come back in another, or reversing directions so people don't get lopsided, and so on. But remember the main idea is simply to avoid collisions.

Traffic in a pool follows many of the same rules as regular highways and byways—stay right of the lane divider and keep out of your fellow swimmer's way!

Who goes first? Now that we've taken care of head-on collisions, let's deal with the other kind—rear-enders. Under *nearly* all conditions, the fastest swimmer *for this particular part* of the workout should go first. (You'll see in a moment why there are so many qualifiers in that sentence.) The rest leave five or ten seconds after the person ahead of them.

We said "for this particular part" to remind you that just because a person goes first on a freestyle set, it doesn't mean that he or she is "first in this lane," anymore than it means that this is "my" lane. Obviously, the fastest breaststroke kicker should go first on a breaststroke kicking set, the faster backstroker on a backstroke set, and so on.

We said "nearly all conditions" because there are workouts when a slower swimmer will take a big head start and the faster swimmer will then try to catch up, a grown-up version of tag. Or the faster swimmer may be warming up or warming down and trying to stay out of everyone's way by going last.

But what if the workout has you doing your best stroke down and your worst stroke back? *You* crash into your lane partner on the first length if *he* or *she* goes first, and he or she crashes into you on the way back if *you* go first? The solution is to let whichever person has the fastest *combined* time go first, and the second person wait for a longer time before taking off—say, ten or even fifteen seconds. That way, neither person interferes with the other person's swim. (Remember the Golden Rule?)

You're expected to work these things out among the people in your lane—"You go first, okay? I dropped a bowling ball on my foot last weekend, and I'm not going to be kicking very hard."

Passing, turns, and so on: What happens when the person who went first swam too fast at the beginning and now you're almost hitting his feet with every stroke as he slows down? The whole point of all of the above is to avoid having two people in the same spot at the same time, but it happens sometimes.

Passing is one of the most unpleasant, undesirable, and dangerous things swimmers do in a workout. If you're aware that the person behind you is catching up, why not pull over at the next turn and let him or her go by? If someone's getting in your way, a tap on the feet should let the swimmer know you're there so he or she can let you by.

Sure, it's fun to be competitive—but not when it interferes with someone else's workout. If you have a problem on a repeat, work something out with the other person to keep it from happening on the next one. The other person should go first, or the second one should give the first one a longer head start.

One other thing. Do everyone a favor and don't hang on the wall right over the target when someone else is swimming. If you must stay in the lane, squeeze over into the corner so the other people have enough room to make their turns.

Some Other Basic Rules

Other points of swimming etiquette don't have much to do with traffic patterns but are still very important for keeping things running smoothly:

Listen to your coach. Whether your coach has dozens of years of experience coaching national champions, or is a summer lifeguard trying to make some extra money while school is out, making things runs smoothly for *everyone* is that person's responsibility.

Most coaches who've dealt with adult swimmers know that they're quite different to coach than youngsters. They have all sorts of other commitments in their lives, as well as more physical problems and schedule conflicts. If you want to do something different—you dropped a bowling ball on your foot and you don't want to kick—check with the coach. They can be very accommodating much of the time, but they can't always comply. The more crowded the pool is, the less room they have for flexibility.

Be on time. In most cases, if you're a few minutes late, everyone understands—but don't expect to do the whole workout from the start. Swim whatever set everyone else in the lane is doing and use that as your warm-up, going last in the lane until you've swum your normal warm-up distance.

A few clubs have so many members that they can't afford to let people walk in whenever it's convenient. If you aren't on time, you don't get to swim. But even if your club is more flexible, try to be on time. Not only does it show courtesy to your coach and the other swimmers, but you'll get a better workout.

Jargon Demystified

Now you're on time and in the right lane, and you're ready to start swimming. The coach comes by and says something that sounds like "five one hundreds klurs on two fifteen descend" and walks away. *What?!?*

There's a lot of jargon involved in describing a swimming workout. Let's discuss *distances* first. A typical training pool, the kind found at high schools, many community centers, YMCA's, and country clubs, is twenty-five yards long. The official Olympic and international competition pool is fifty meters long, and these are much rarer. And *much* longer. Fifty meters is about fifty-five yards, and looks like half a mile the first time you swim in one.

Hotels, condominiums, and community centers often call their pools "Olympic-sized" when what they really mean is "This one's too big for a backyard." Many pools, especially those built before modern rules came into effect, are odd distances. You may find twenty-yard pools, twenty-five-meter pools, fifty-yard pools, fifty-five-yard pools (which are different enough from fifty meters to be illegal for 'international competition), and even 33⅓- and 66⅔-yard pools, and many of them will be promoted as "Olympic-sized."

Swimmers always refer to swims in terms of *distance* rather than the *number of lengths*. When the coach comes over and tells you to swim a hundred, he means a hundred yards, not a hundred lengths. A hundred yards is only four lengths of a twenty-five-yard pool. Swimmers rarely say "laps" because that implies down *and back*, or *two* lengths to some people.

A day's workout is broken into a few large sections called *sets*, and each set is divided into several "swims" or "repeats." These repeated swims that make up a set are done on a certain "interval" of time.

Let's look at a typical set. After you've warmed up, your coach might tell you to do eight one hundreds free on two minutes. On a chalkboard, it might look like this:

$$8 \times 100 \text{ fr @ } 2:00$$

Translated into everyday English this means:

$8 \times$ = do the following eight times:
100 fr = four lengths of freestyle (crawl)
@ 2:00 = starting a new 100 every two minutes

If it takes you 1:45 (a minute and forty-five seconds) to swim four lengths of freestyle, this means you will get fifteen seconds to rest before you start the next one. (If any of these times sound awfully fast or awfully slow, don't panic—they're just examples. Your coach will get to know what intervals you can handle and put you in a lane with others of similar ability.)

This type of interval is called a *send-off interval* because it measures the time between the starts (send-offs) of successive repeats. The other type is the *rest interval,* which measures the time between the *end* of one repeat and the *start* of the next one. With a ten-second rest interval, you get ten seconds whether you swim your 100 yards in fifty-five seconds or a week and a half. Rest intervals are usually written with *RI* or *rest* after them, like this:

$$5 \times 100 \text{ fly @ } 30 \text{ RI}$$

Rest intervals are less common for two reasons. First of all, swimmers will gradually get "out of sync" in a crowded lane because some are faster than others. It doesn't take long before the faster ones and the slower ones are getting in each other's way.

The other reason is that coaches know most people will work harder if they're under pressure to "make their interval." If you are doing 100s on two minutes and just barely holding 1:55, you'll keep trying to get back in time to start the next repeat. On the other hand, if you're going to get the same amount of rest no matter when you finish, you may figure, "Why kill myself, right?"

So if you are told an interval to do, you can assume it's a send-off interval unless you're specifically told otherwise.

YOUR FIRST WORKOUT

Let's look at the basic structure of a workout. Every workout is a variation on a simple format: a warm-up, the main set or sets, and the warm-down.

The warm-up: Some coaches will have you do your own warm-up and leave the details up to you or just tell you to swim a certain distance, say 400 yards. But most coaches begin the workout with a set specifically designed to warm you up— a warm-up set.

If you start swimming hard without a warm-up, you put a much greater strain on your body, and chances are much higher that you will injure yourself, or at the very least, be unusually sore the next day. Warm-ups prepare your body for the workout to come by relaxing your muscles, filling them with blood and oxygen, and making them warm and lubricated. A warm-up set is usually a series of swims on an interval long enough that you can swim at a relaxed pace without feeling hurried. This is not the time to swim fast. Take your time and ease into it. If you have any sort of physical problems like a bad back or joint injury, be especially careful to warm up thoroughly. Sometimes warm-ups include more than one set and you may do some kicking, stroke drills, or even a few sprints toward the end of the warm-up.

The main set or sets: Once you've warmed up, it's time to begin the hard work that's designed to get you into better shape, make you stronger, and improve your technique. In a moment, we'll look at several things that can be varied—the pace, time, distances, and strokes—to keep you challenged and interested. The variations can be combined in so many ways, you may never have to suffer through a boring workout!

The warm-down: Many swimmers will hop out of the pool after the last main set, and then wonder why they're so sore the next morning. Strenuous exercise produces a lot of waste products in your muscles. If you exercise gently for a few minutes afterward, you help your system break these waste products down. Otherwise they continue to do damage even after you've stopped exercising.

Pulling yourself out of the water, standing up, and moving into an air temperature different from the water can put an extra load on a heart that has already been working hard. Many exercise-related heart attacks don't happen during exercise—they happen right *after*. A warm-down can help prevent this. Swim easily and gently, stretching your muscles and breathing deeply until your heart rate has slowed to well below your Target Heart Rate.

SPICING UP YOUR DAILY ROUTINE

While one of the main reasons for dividing a workout into smaller sets of repeated swims is to increase the workout's physical benefits for your cardiovascular system, technique, and strength, a little bit of *creativity* in designing those sets can go a long way toward keeping you motivated and preventing boredom. Let's take a look at ways we can have some fun with our intervals.

Pace Variations

Straight and pace sets: These are sets in which you swim at a steady speed through the whole set. For instance, you may be asked to swim 8 × 100 (that's one hundred yards, eight times) with a two-minute send-off. If you keep your times all within a few seconds of each other, you are swimming *straight*. Because maintaining an even pace is important in distance swimming, this type of set is sometimes referred to as a *pace set*.

Descending and negative splitting: These two are similar enough that people often confuse them. Both of them mean "going faster," but there is a difference.

As we saw in our discussion of the twelve-minute test, a split is your time for a *part* of a single swim. *Negative splitting* means making the second half (or split) of each repeat faster than the first half. If you swim 4 × 200 negative split, you are supposed to swim the second half of *each* 200 faster than the first half. How do you know if you're going faster? Sneak a peek at the pace clock as you turn. Otherwise, you have to just rely on your own sense of "pace."

Descending, on the other hand, refers to *successive* swims. To descend 4 × 200, you would make *each* 200 faster than the

200 before. For instance, if your first 200 was 3:36, then you would try to go faster on the second one—let's say you swim 3:32. Then you try to beat that time for your third one, and so on.

Negative splitting and descending both mean going faster, but each does it in a different way. When you *negative split*, you go faster *during* a swim. When you *descend*, you go faster *from one swim to the next.*

Building: Building also means going faster, but you do it gradually throughout each repeat until you're going as fast as you can at the very end. This variation is especially helpful for learning to swim fast with good technique. Most of us can swim beautifully at a gentle pace; if we then try to accelerate gradually, we will carry that form into our faster swimming. Many coaches recommend building as the way to learn pace for the middle distance swims like 200s and 500s.

Fartlek: This Swedish word meaning "speed play" was popularized by runners, and although it's less common in swimming, you may still come across it. The variations we've discussed so far are all different types of fartlek training. While "descending" or "negative splitting" will mean the same thing from one coach to another, *fartlek* isn't a standard term. If your coach uses the term fartlek, ask him or her exactly what it means. He or she may just mean to vary your speed at will.

Time Variations

Decreasing interval sets: On these, your send-off time is shortened, meaning you have less and less time to rest from one swim to the next. Let's look at 5 × 100 on an interval that decreases by five seconds. If you started on a 2:10 interval for the first one, you would do the next one on a 2:05 interval, then 2:00. Just keeping track of when you're supposed to go next can be a real challenge!

Decreasing intervals are often used for warm-ups—as you become more warmed-up, you have to swim faster. You might also find decreasing interval sets later in the workout. Here they are often *open-ended*, meaning your interval keeps decreasing until it's so short you finally miss the send-off for the next swim. These challenging sets can be very exciting and many clubs have special names for favorite ones, often naming them after the swimmer or coach who invented them.

Broken swims: The last time variation we'll look at is stopping for a short time in the *middle* of a swim. This rest is usually just long enough for you to look at the clock and grab a few breaths. Here's an example:

$$3 \times 200 \text{ @ } 3:45 \text{ broken } 10$$

This still means swimming 200 yards three times, with a three-minute, forty-five-second send-off, but the difference is the "broken 10"—you stop for ten seconds halfway through each 200; the swim is broken into two parts. This variation:

$$3 \times 200 \text{ @ } 3:45 \text{ broken } 10 \text{ each } 50$$

means you stop for ten seconds after each fifty—every two lengths.

Broken swims are usually combined with something else. For instance, you may be asked to negative split (the break gives you a good chance to see the clock), sprint the last fifty, take fewer breaths the second part, or hold a consistent pace for each half. You may even be asked to descend successive broken swims!

Distance Variations

Swimming 10×100 gets pretty boring after a while, even if you use the time variations above. Here are a couple of other ways to break up 1,000 yards:

$$5 \times 200$$

$$20 \times 50$$

Still too boring? Each of the following sets also totals 1,000 yards:

$$100\text{–}400 \text{ ladder by } 100\text{s}$$

50–200, 200–50 pyramid by 50s

1 × 200
2 × 150
3 × 100
4 × 50

4 × (3 × 50, 1 × 100)

50–200 locomotion

Now that's more interesting, isn't it? But what does it all mean?

Ladders and pyramids: In ladder sets, the distance increases and/or decreases. You climb up or down the ladder as you go. The first set above is a ladder that goes up. You swim a 100, then a 200, then a 300, and finally a 400.

Since the second set is a ladder that goes up and back down, this type is also known as a *pyramid.* You start with a fifty, then add fifty yards each time until you've reached 200. Then you do another 200 and start back down, subtracting fifty yards each time. A popular variation is remembering your times for each swim as you go up the ladder and trying to beat each one on the way back down. This is "descending on the way down."

The third set is another ladder variation. This time, as the distances get shorter, you do more of them.

The fourth set is a real mixed bag—a set within a set. You start by swimming three 50s and then one 100, and you repeat that *set* (3 × 50, 1 × 100) a total of four times.

Locomotion: Locomotion (or its diminutive, *loco*) is a less standardized term, but it usually signifies a combination of ladders *and* speed play. Ask your coach to explain if he or she tells you to do a "50 to 200 loco." It's probably something like the following: "Swim a fifty hard and a fifty easy, then a 100 hard and a 100 easy, then a 150 hard and a 150 easy, and then a 200 hard and a 200 easy." (See why some people call it "loco"?)

Stroke Variations

Changing strokes is one obvious way to put more variety

into workouts. This has other benefits, too. Doing the other strokes improves your feel for the water, your skills, your strength and endurance. Here are some samples:

Your choice, specialty, or stroke sets: This means that each swimmer is free to choose what stroke or strokes to do for the set. For example, "8 × 50 your choice down, freestyle back" means do whatever stroke you want the first twenty-five yards and freestyle on the second length. When some coaches say "stroke" or "your choice," they may mean anything *but* freestyle. The term *specialty* has the additional implication that you are supposed to do your *best* stroke.

Individual medley (IM) sets: In the individual medley race, each swimmer does all four of the strokes in a specific order—butterfly, backstroke, breaststroke, and freestyle—and variations on the IM are common stroke sets. Your coach may have you do them in reverse order, leave off free or one of the other strokes, or do the first or second half by itself, and so on.

Drills: Drills may be worked right into the middle of a set. Doing one set of 5 × 50 kick and one set of 10 x 100 free is like eating *all* of your vegetables and then *all* of your steak. Instead, you might do:

5 × (2 × 100 swim, 1 × 50 kick)

It's the same amount of swimming and kicking, but more interesting. Likewise, your coach may have you insert some KLRS (Kick the first length, Left arm only the second, Right arm the third, and Swim the last), breathing drills, or similar variations in a long set.

Breath control, lung-busters, and hypoxic swimming: It was originally thought that making athletes hold their breath while training would make their blood adapt to carry more oxygen, but subsequent research hasn't given the theory much support. On the other hand, it does seem to make swimmers go faster.

Why? Any time you can challenge an athlete in training, you will probably see an improvement—and trying to swim fast while holding one's breath can be *very* challenging. Being able to hold your breath well comes in handy on starts and turns, too, and in sprints, fewer breaths often mean faster times, because taking lots of breaths slows down most swimmers.

On the negative side, a person's lungs will involuntarily try to breathe when the blood's carbon dioxide level reaches a certain point. This can be a problem if you're several feet below the surface at the time. For this reason, many coaches don't allow underwater swimming contests. If you do any underwater swimming, it should only be with very close supervision.

The form that breath control or hypoxic swimming usually takes is a set called *200 lung-busters.* You start out breathing every three strokes, counting each arm as one stroke. After two lengths, you breathe every *five* strokes. Then, after two more lengths, you change to every *seven* strokes, and finally every *nine* strokes for the last two lengths.

Some swimmers love the challenge of lung-busters. Swimming a fast set of LBs takes courage and leaves them with a nice feeling of accomplishment afterwards. On the other hand, some people *hate* hypoxic swimming. It can cause headaches and even nausea in some people. Others just plain don't like feeling that much breathing discomfort when they're in water.

Another form of breath control is taking a fixed number of breaths per length or per repeat. For example, take three breaths per length or twelve breaths per hundred.

Many people slow down right before a turn for one last, big breath or come up gasping for one immediately after, losing the speed advantage of a good turn. For this reason, coaches often tell swimmers to hold their breaths into and away from the wall, allowing no breaths in the five yards between the flags and the wall.

No-breath swimming may also help fix stroke problems related to breathing at the wrong time. Breathing less often will sometimes help the problem cure itself. It also makes it easier to watch your hands and concentrate on what they're doing. Even so, keep in mind that hypoxic training can be dangerous, particularly to older swimmers and those out of shape. Exercise caution. Some coaches are firmly against this sort of breath control, especially when it gets into the challenge of "no-breathers."

In the next chapter, we'll see how these different types of workouts can be combined to accomplish *your* swimming and fitness goals.

6
ONWARD AND UPWARD: ADVANCED TRAINING CONCEPTS

Once you've met your coaches and teammates, learned the terminology, and gotten the hang of participating in workouts, you might find yourself getting restless and wondering, "Is there any way I can get faster results?"

You bet there is! Most swimmers just go to the pool and do the day's workout. We want to give you a little extra headstart on them by showing you *why* practices are structured the way they are and *how* you can reach your goals sooner.

SWIMMING PSYCHOLOGY—SETTING GOALS THAT WORK

The secret to accomplishing anything is *motivation*, and the secret to motivation is *setting goals*. Find something that's important to you, be sure it's realistic, make it concrete, and then chart your course to accomplishing it.

Be honest with yourself. What do you want from swimming? Are you swimming to lose weight, to improve your health, to enjoy that special fellowship athletics creates, or to win "hardware" for your mantel? What is it you like and don't like

The secret to accomplishing anything is motivation, and the secret to motivation is setting goals.

about swimming? Look at the emotional side, too. How do you feel about swimming? How does swimming make you feel?

Make your goal concrete and specific. If you express your goal in a *measurable* form, you can see if you're making progress. If your primary goal is to look and feel healthier, what measurable accomplishment could you shoot for? To lose a certain number of pounds, to fit into a certain size clothing, to bring your cholesterol, blood pressure, or resting heart rate down to a certain level?

Is your goal more performance-oriented? Perhaps you want to be able to swim a mile without stopping, or to swim it under a certain time limit. What time is that, exactly?

Next, break your goal down into a series of smaller check-points. For instance, if your goal is to swim a mile (a "swimmer's mile" of 1,650 yards) under fifty minutes, a little math tells us you need to average about 3:02 for each 100 yards (four lengths). That doesn't sound so bad, does it? You might be able to do that right now. Can you do a 200 on 6:04, or a 400 in twelve minutes? Each of these becomes an intermediate goal to shoot for. Then, once you accomplish that, you might try to do two 400s, each one under twelve minutes.

Gradually, as we begin to nibble away at these smaller goals, we suddenly notice one day that the BIG goal we set so long ago is the next logical, inevitable step. As the Chinese say, even a journey of a thousand miles begins with a single step.

Now that we've got an idea of how to set our goals, let's take a look at how we're going to reach them.

TRAINING AND OVERTRAINING

The answer to "How much should I train?" depends on what you are trying to accomplish. A swimmer aiming to lose ten pounds by the holidays will have a very different regimen from someone shooting for a medal at the National Championships. Here are some guidelines to help you answer the question for yourself.

You should train *at least* three days a week and *at most* six days a week. Remember stress and adaptation? Less than three is too little stress, more than six is too little recovery.

Getting into shape is much harder than *staying in* shape. Research has shown that nearly twice as much training is required to *improve* someone's fitness as to *maintain* it at current levels. It takes just a few weeks to lose nearly all your conditioning and it will seem like forever trying to get it back. Three days a week will save you a lot of hard work later on.

If you do have problems fitting your training into your schedule, other aerobic activities like running, cycling, or even brisk walking will help keep you in shape. Don't get caught in the trap of "all-or-nothing" training. You can find a different pool, or a different time, or just do part of a workout if you have scheduling problems. A twenty-minute workout is far better than no workout at all.

Many people, rather than wondering how much training is enough, find themselves having problems with *too* much training. Too much stress or too little rest can cause what the scientists call "a failure of adaptation." Athletes and coaches call it *"overtraining."* Overtraining can lower your resistance and make you more susceptible to injury.

Listen to your body and get to know your own warning signs. In Chapter Four, we mentioned checking your heart rate each morning before you get out of bed—a sudden increase of more than 10 percent one day can be a sign that you haven't recovered from your last workout yet. You may find even better personal indicators, though, like nervousness, a feeling of malaise, or insomnia. Some people know they're overdoing it when they feel like crying for no reason or become irritable with their families. Or just plain hate swimming!

Any of these signals can mean you should cut back on your intensity or distance, or get more rest. Don't get caught up in having to do so-many yards this week or keep a perfect attendance record. Your health is much more important.

THE THREE ENERGY SYSTEMS

Your muscles have three main systems for producing energy, and physiologists divide athletic events into three types based on the type of energy that predominates. These are:

1. Sprints, which generally last less than a minute;

2. Middle-distance events, which last from about one minute to about three minutes;

3. Distance events, which last more than three minutes.

The sprints use instant energy that's stored right in your muscles, ready for immediate use. Unfortunately, it's in very limited supply.

As your body uses up this instant energy, the *anaerobic* (oxygen-less) system begins to take over. This middle-distance system can supply energy almost as fast as the sprint system, but it has a nasty by-product: *lactic acid*. Lactic acid is produced when there isn't enough oxygen to carry the chemical breakdown of fuel all the way to water and carbon dioxide and you go into *oxygen debt*. It burns your muscles because it's an *acid* and eventually, the burning becomes so intense you have to stop. The third system, used in distance events, is the *aerobic* energy system. If we pace ourselves so that our muscles aren't consuming oxygen faster than our cardiovascular systems can supply it, lactic acid won't accumulate. It produces energy much more slowly, but it will go on for as long as there is fuel (mostly stored carbohydrate and some fat) to be burned.

The energy we have available for exercise is very similar to money. The first system, the sprinting system, is like *cash*. When you need to spend some, it's right there, ready. But most of us don't carry very much cash. The second system, the middle-distance energy system, is more like a credit card. Don't have enough cash? No problem—charge it! But there's a limit on this energy just like there's a limit on your credit card. Bump up against that limit, and you have to stop. The third system, the distance system, is more like a *budget*. You know how much you can spend, based on how much comes in. If you keep track of your budget and pace your spending, you could go on indefinitely and still have plenty of cash and credit handy when you need them.

SPECIFICITY

Since we have three energy systems, we need three different types of training. This is due to *specificity*. All this technical term really means is that your body is going to adapt best to the *specific* stress you put on it.

Spending all your time swimming distance workouts won't help your sprinting ability very much. It may help your running or bicycling some, because your heart is getting a good workout, but don't expect it to do a lot for your tennis. If you're a pole-vaulter, you can forget about any carry-over.

Different people have different mental and physical predispositions for sprinting or distance swimming. But whether you're a sprinter, middle-distance, or distance swimmer deep down inside, *everyone* should do a combination of all three types of training in workouts.

ADJUSTING YOUR INTERVALS FOR THE THREE ENERGY SYSTEMS

The basic concept behind training is to adjust your intensity and rest so the specific energy system you want to work on is affected.

Remember your Target Heart Rate Zone (THR) we helped you find earlier? You can use it to discover what type of workout you are getting. (Obviously, the maximum intensity efforts and high heart rates we'll discuss here apply only to well-conditioned athletes.)

Training for distance means training your heart, lungs, and circulatory system to deliver more oxygen to your muscles. A typical distance workout involves longer swims with shorter rest periods. If you've been lap-swimming up until now, you've been doing a particular type of distance training known as *long, slow distance*—LSD, for short.

Long, slow distance is also known as *overdistance* because you are swimming farther than the distance of most races. The other main type of endurance training is *short-rest interval* training. In both of these, your heart rate will remain at a nearly constant level, in the middle-to-lower end of your THR Zone. The amount of rest time will be very short compared to the swimming time. Many swimmers who become obsessed with the quantity of yards they've swum each day rely on this type of swimming almost exclusively. They may get a great workout for their cardiovascular systems, but they're not going to develop much speed.

Middle-distance swimming is *anaerobic*, creating lactic acid, that burning sensation you get in your muscles when you go into oxygen debt. The goal is to learn to tolerate lactic acid better while training your body to deliver more oxygen. In order to do this, you have to swim fast enough to cross over your anaerobic threshold into oxygen debt.

Middle-distance workouts have longer rests than distance workouts—from roughly thirty seconds to a minute or so— and the swims are of higher intensity. The distance of each swim will be relatively short—200 yards at the most, and usually much less. A swimmer's heart rate will go up near the top of the THR Zone, and even exceed it toward the end of the set.

Speed-play variations are very common in this type of workout—descending, building, negative splitting, or alternating hard and easy swims. The heart rate is allowed to drop during the rests and easy swims, down near the bottom of the THR Zone or even a bit lower. Remember that middle-distance races create lactic acid. The amount of burning you experience in your muscles is a good gauge of how much of a middle-distance, anaerobic workout you are getting.

Sprint workouts are sets of short, maximum-intensity efforts with very long rests in between that allow the heart rate to return back to near normal before the next effort. The rests will be much longer than the swims. Sometimes coaches will even have sprinters swimming distances as short as 12½ yards, to encourage them to hold absolutely nothing back and get a feeling of truly going all out.

QUALITY AND QUANTITY

Every swimmer interested in better swimming should practice all three types of training—sprints, middle-distance, and distance. No swimmer should use the same intervals day in and day out, even though you often hear comments such as, "What's your interval in this lane?" Your body adapts very quickly, and if you use the same interval all the time your workouts will become less and less productive.

Distance training is the least harmful to your body in the long run. Your heart stays within your Target Heart Rate zone and your muscles and joints are less prone to injury because they're under less strain. Aerobic exercise also has many psychological benefits.

On the other hand, a swimmer doing nothing but distance training can develop many sloppy stroke habits. Watch a championship meet sometime and pay attention to the strokes in the different distances. The longer the race is, the more you'll see idiosyncratic strokes.

Sprinting can have very beneficial effects on your technique, even if you have little interest in becoming a better sprinter. Doing occasional sprints in practice can make you a better distance swimmer by making your stroke more efficient.

Middle-distance training helps both sprinters and distance swimmers. Sprinters learn to finish strongly, by increasing their tolerance for the lactic acid which begins to accumulate toward the end of their race. Distance swimmers benefit from middle-distance training because crossing over the anaerobic threshold creates an adaptation pressure to bring more oxygen in and turn the *anaerobic* swim into an *aerobic* one. Middle-distance training helps improve your endurance *and* your technique.

Distance training should be the backbone of any training program. It's like an insurance policy, building protection against injury and preparing the heart, joints, and muscles for the even greater stresses of swimming hard for shorter distances. For that reason, distance training is especially important when you're first getting into shape.

Middle-distance and sprint swimming put much greater demands on the body, and therefore can't be done as much or as often as distance swimming.

Athletes and coaches often make a distinction between quality and quantity training. *Quality* training means that you are swimming near race pace, with good technique and concentration. *Quantity* training means concentrating on the distance—long swims with little rest and lap-swimming.

While quantity training puts less strain on your body, quality swimming produces bigger improvements in less time. You have to watch for signs of overtraining, though, because it's more stressful. Try to strike a balance between the two.

A DAY'S WORKOUT

Since sprinting and middle-distance swimming make high demands on your body, you need to be sure you've warmed up adequately before doing them. Many coaches will save the really fast swimming until the end of the workout for this reason.

On the other hand, distance training can seem almost like an extension of your warm-up. You start out slowly, with plenty of rest, gradually start swimming faster, with shorter rests, and soon you're in your Target Heart Rate Zone. So not only should *most* of your workout be distance swimming, but the sprinting and middle-distance training should be saved until you're warmed up.

However, if it's the end of the workout, you're tired, your

stroke has gotten sloppy, and you're thinking about getting to the office or picking up the kids, you probably won't get much out of a sprinting set—you'll just cruise it at your aerobic pace. The best time to do quality sets may be either right after a long warm-up or in the middle of a workout while you're still fresh.

A WEEK'S SCHEDULE

Just as there are ways of balancing faster and slower swimming into each day's workouts, a balance should be made over the course of a week.

If your workout days fall back to back, it's wise to be careful not to overdo the speed swimming on the second day. Since it's a greater stress, the recovery time needed is longer too. This is something to keep in mind if you're involved in other types of physical activities such as cycling or running. You might be able to do tough workouts on consecutive days if you aren't stressing the same muscle groups. A long, easy run after a hard day of swimming allows you to continue aerobic training without risking overuse injury; highly skilled athletes also find that a hard workout in another sport the following day maximizes results by stressing different systems. In any case, beware of overtraining. When combining sports, try to strike a balance between hard and easy workouts.

PLANNING A SEASON

What is a season? Ordinarily, a season is the time between one championship meet and the next. For Masters, the Short Course season (events swum in a twenty-five-yard pool) runs from roughly late August to mid-May, and the Long Course season (events swum in a fifty-meter pool) is the rest of the year.

But you can think of a season as the period from when you decide to aim for a goal, and the time you're finally tested. *Your* season may be entirely different from someone else's. Perhaps you've decided you'd really like to try an open-water event in July, and you start planning and training for it in January. Those six months are your season.

Just as each day's workout should have a warm-up when you prepare for the work ahead, a middle section when you do the serious training, and a warm-down at the end to let your body recover, a season has a *base*, a *building phase*, and a *taper*.

A Solid Foundation

A season, like a house, should be built on a firm foundation. That foundation consists of establishing good technique and building your endurance for the training to come.

Few things are as potentially disastrous as trying to make a major change in a swimmer's technique any time close to a big event. There's a period of *unlearning* the old habits and *relearning* the new ones, and the length of time can be very unpredictable. Meanwhile, the swimmer will be *slower* than before. So if you're planning changes in your technique, such as learning flip turns, bilateral breathing, or changing your backstroke head position, work on them well in advance.

Building endurance is a slower process than building sprinting speed, and so requires a head start. Increasing your quantity of yardage first, before incorporating speed work into your training, also helps decrease the likelihood of injuries, heart attacks, and other problems that exertion can cause.

Swimmers often refer to the beginning of the season as their *base*, the time they are building the foundation on which the entire season will rest. You may hear remarks such as, "We're concentrating on our base for the next four weeks," and, "He did so well because he had so much base yardage."

Building

Once you've established a solid base, you build on it. If your main focus is the open-water swimming season, you'll start to lean more and more in that direction, concentrating on distance training (but not exclusively) and gaining experience in open conditions. If your big event will be swimming backstroke on a medley relay team at the local championships, you'll start tailoring your training to reach that goal.

This is the time when the sprinters begin to work more quality training into their workouts, when the stroke specialists begin to put more and more time in on their specialty, and the rough-water swimmers and triathletes begin to get that crazy gleam in their eyes.

Building is when overtraining is most likely to rear its ugly head, the time when people start becoming "serious." Remember to increase your yardage and intensity gradually. If you find yourself wondering if you're overdoing it, you probably are!

The Taper

All season long, you've kept one step ahead of your body, asking it to adapt to ever-increasing stresses. As you become faster and stronger, you continue training harder, being careful not to step over that line into *over*training. The natural result of all this is that most of the time, you're a little tired and sore. Then, a couple of weeks before the big meet, you decrease the intensity and the distance—you begin to *taper*.

When an athlete allows his or her body to finally catch up to all the months of hard work, amazing things can happen. It's not at all unusual for people to improve their best times by

Training with others makes workouts challenging and fun.

several seconds in the longer races when all that tiredness and soreness is finally, completely gone.

During this time, the total amount of swimming will be cut way back, and workouts may feel more like parties than workouts. People come to the pool, loosen up, and then swim just enough to keep their "edge." There's nothing you can do in the last week or two to get into better shape; the last several months have already determined that.

This period is sometimes referred to as fine-tuning. Between an easy warm-up and warm-down, nearly all the rest of the swimming will be done near race speed to get the feel and pace right. Concentrate on the details of your events, the starts and turns, decide exactly what warm-up to use on race-day, what you'll eat the day before, and so on.

People have different reactions to tapering. Many feel very energetic and excited about the big race coming up. All that background fatigue disappears, they see their times in practice dropping and they feel great!

Others may worry about cutting back on their workouts and become anxious. That increased energy turns into nervousness. If this happens to you, just remember that it's a common

Supplement your swimming with such dry-land equipment as the isokinetic swim bench, which allows you to simulate swimming motions.

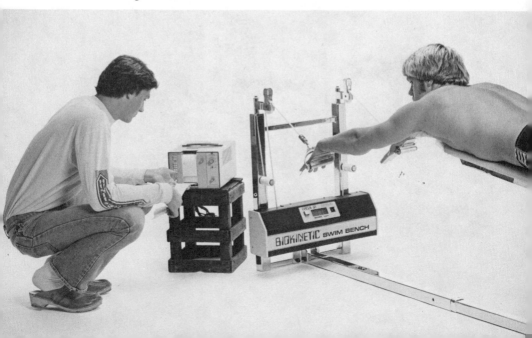

reaction, and a lot of the jitteriness you're feeling is energy released by your taper. You'll do fine!

DRY-LAND TRAINING

There are other training techniques that can help improve your swimming without your even getting wet. They fall into two main areas—flexibility and strength training—and are often lumped together as *dry-land training*.

All you need is to watch a good breaststroker's ankle movement or a champion butterflier's stroke to know that swimming requires a lot of flexibility. As we get older, we get stiffer and a regular stretching program should be part of any adult swimmer's routine.

If you stretch at the *end* of your workout, when your muscles are loose and warm, you'll get a better stretch with less chance of injury. Push to the point of discomfort—not *pain*—and hold. No bouncing!

Some of the best stretches require a helper. Don't be shy, ask. It's an old swimming tradition—you stretch me, I'll stretch you.

Weight Training

Despite the fact that all collegiate, national, and Olympic champions use weights, many people still believe the myth that weight training is bad for swimmers, making them muscle-bound—bulky and stiff.

Most myths have an element of truth in them, and this one's no exception. Weight training *can* make you bulky and stiff, but only when you do it the wrong way. Done properly, weight training builds more than strength. It improves your flexibility, your neuromuscular coordination, and the way your body stores and burns fuel. It also protects you from injuries.

It doesn't have to take a huge bite out of your already crowded schedule, either. A half hour of lifting twice a week, with ten to fifteen minutes of stretching and loosening up before *and* after, can produce definite results. That's only two hours a week!

One set of eight to twelve repetitions for each exercise

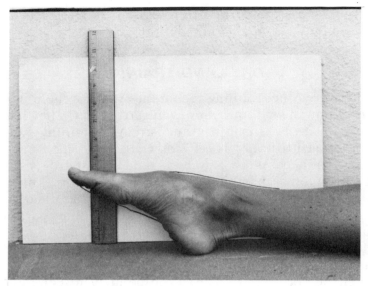

Test your progress from time to time in "ankle flexibility." Some swimmers will occasionally sit back on their heels to stretch their ankles out. Have a friend trace the arc of your foot, and measure your improvement!

strengthens tendons, stabilizes joints, and trains muscle groups to fire in better synchronization. Fewer reps and you're building bulk you won't want to push through the water. More, and you're training aerobically—time that's better spent in the water.

Be especially alert for overtraining, and warm up and down thoroughly. You can save time by doing weights right after a regular workout when you're already warmed up.

7
THE BIG TIME: MASTERS SWIMMING

Well, you've been swimming your workouts for a while now and getting pretty good. Want to know how good? Why not go to a Masters meet and find out? It's a great way to get feedback on your progress, meet new people, and spend a wonderful day outdoors.

"Oh, no," you say, "I'm not interested in competition."

It's a shame that the main thing keeping many of us from enjoying the fun of a swim meet is fear of embarrassment. Meets are structured so that everyone gets to race with others of the same speed. Don't worry that you'll still be stroking away while those superstars on your team have already dried off. You'll be in a different heat (group of six competitors).

If you competed when you were younger, and your memories are full of tension, disappointment, and pushy parents and coaches, you're in for a real treat. Masters swimming can be as laid back as *you* want it to be. Go on down, have some fun. And say hello to some wonderful memories in the making.

Masters is *people*, and the camaraderie and excitement are the main reasons that many of us go to meets. Lifelong friendships can be formed just on the basis of one race where

The wonderful thing about Masters swimming is the camaraderie.

the two of you inspire each other to discover inner strengths you never knew you had.

For many of us, knowing there's a meet coming up motivates us to train even more diligently, and the fun and excitement of the meet itself is a great shot in the arm, renewing our enthusiasm for weeks and weeks.

The main goal of Masters competition is encouraging people to participate. Male and female swimmers are divided into five-year age groups starting with 20-24, continuing all the way up from 25-29, to 30-34, to 75-79, and 90-and-over so more people can win awards. National Championships are open to *all* registered Masters swimmers, not just to those who meet certain time standards or qualify in regional meets.

If you're still not convinced that you really ought to give it a try, read on. In a moment, we'll show you low-key ways to get into competition and some special events designed so that you don't even have to go anywhere to compete!

THE HISTORY OF MASTERS SWIMMING

Until recently, adult swimmers wanting to compete had nowhere to go. Swimming was very organized from as early as ages five and six on up through high school and college athletics. Beyond college, though, the only program available was *senior* swimming. The term *seniors* can confuse newcomers—it definitely does not mean senior citizen! Seniors are what little kids graduate into from the age-group program—the Olympic teams are the best of the senior swimmers. Obviously, the training and ability required to compete at the senior level are beyond what most adults can muster.

The lack of an adult competition program was another example of the Puritan Ethic and the Spectator Mentality at work in our lives. Why would any grown-up want to play a kid's game? And even if a person did, why would you bother unless you could still be the best? Most professional athletes have the dignity to retire before they begin that inevitable, depressing, and ultimately degrading decline in performance that comes with age. They know when to quit.

This unhealthy attitude disregards the fact that sports and competition are *fun*, no matter what your age. Nowadays we are accustomed to seeing retired people out jogging in the early morning hours and senior citizens setting out on bicycle camping tours hundreds of miles long. Masters divisions have sprung up in many sports, proof that there are many adults in this world who would rather do than watch.

Masters Swimming was founded in 1968 by Dr. Ransom J. Arthur, an officer in the Navy Medical Corps, to encourage participation, fun, and physical fitness. In May 1970, the first Masters National Championships were held in Amarillo, Texas, organized by John Spannuth, who was then the director of the Amarillo Aquatic Club and president of the American Swim Coaches Association. Forty-nine people competed in that first Masters Nationals, and the sport has grown to the point where there are now over 17,000 registered Masters swimmers. A typical Short Course National Championship attracts over 1,200 participants.

National records are kept for men and women in each age group, and each season a list of each age group's Top Ten

Times for all the events is published. All-Americans are also named in each age group for the fastest time that season in each event. Local organizations also keep records, publish top-ten lists, and name Swimmers of the Year for outstanding contributions.

One of the great attractions of Masters competition—for both the seasoned competitor *and* the neophyte—is that the emphasis is on fun. People whose memories of childhood competition are filled with pressure are pleasantly surprised to discover how relaxed, sociable, and enjoyable Masters meets can be, and the people who are new to competition are generally delighted to find everyone so patient, supportive, and understanding.

Although Masters swimming is administered nationally by United States Masters Swimming (which took over from the Amateur Athletic Union in 1980), the backbone of Masters is the fifty Local Masters Swim Committees (LMSCs), associations which oversee the Masters teams in their areas. Each season, the LMSCs arrange a schedule of meets sponsored by the clubs. Regional championship meets are held toward the end of the season, and each season culminates with a National Championship meet. Nationals are scheduled in different parts of the country from year to year so everyone has a better opportunity to experience the thrill of competing in a "big meet."

In many sports, a system like this would be used to qualify athletes to compete in the next level. If you achieved a certain time standard at the local level, you could go to the regional championships, and if you placed in the top finishers at regionals, you'd be eligible to go to Nationals. Masters swimming does not operate like this. *Any* registered Masters swimmer can compete at *any* level, up to and including the National Championships. When the Masters national charter says that their primary purpose is to encourage participation, they mean it.

If you've ever secretly wished that you could get a little taste of what it's like to be an Olympian, you can. The next World Masters Games, which, like the Olympics, will include track and field, volleyball, cycling, and a long list of other sports, will be held in Japan in 1987. In the Masters tradition, the games will be open to any registered Masters athlete. Start saving your pennies!

EASY AND LOW-KEY

Maybe we're getting ahead of ourselves—a World Championship may sound a bit over your head at this point. Where can you find a relatively painless introduction to competition?

There are lots of opportunities, once you know where to look. If you've joined a Masters team, tell your coach and teammates you're interested in attending a meet. (If you're unsure of yourself, you could go and watch. Volunteer to be a timer. Some meets accept *deck* entries from people who haven't entered in advance, so be sure to take your suit along in case you decide to get in on the fun.)

Although larger Masters meets are always *open* meets (that is, open to any registered Masters swimmer from any team), you may run across various other formats. Many of these other types of meets can be an ideal way to get introduced to competition. Occasionally, an unofficial intrasquad meet will be organized by a team specifically for introducing its members to competition, with time spent going over the details of how to enter a meet, how meets are run, and the technical rules about starts, turns, relays. If two teams get together to have a meet that's only open to members from the two teams, it's known as a *dual* meet, and there are sometimes *tri* and *quad* meets.

You don't have to go to a Masters meet at all to swim in competition. If you have children on an age-group or country club team, you may have a chance to swim in a *novelty* event. *Family relays* are a lot of fun—everyone on each relay team has to be related and the total of their ages can't exceed a certain figure.

YMCAs have always been at the forefront of adult fitness, and they've long had a YMCA Masters division in competitive swimming. While they require a separate registration (you have to be a Y member), YMCA Masters is very much like USMS Masters, with National Championships, National Records, and so on. If you're already a member of a local Y, see if they have a team.

SOMETHING NEW AND DIFFERENT

Sometimes you might be lucky enough to find what we'll call a *novelty* meet, something a bit unusual, like an all-relay meet, an all-distances events meet, or a meet with a comedy-diving show or synchronized swimming performance in the lunch break.

These special meets have a wonderful way of bringing out the best in swimming and swimmers, and many competitors' fondest memories are of the people they met and things they did at events like these. You can swim on a lot of relays, but how often do you have to stop at the turn and chug down a can of beer before you can swim back, with all of your teammates standing there yelling at you to drink it faster? When was the last time you had to pull a T-shirt off the person ahead of you, put it on and swim to the other end of the pool with this huge, wet, shirt dragging on your arms, only to take it off again so your teammate could climb into it?

The Twenty-Two-Cent Race

Would you believe us if we told you that you didn't even have to go anywhere in order to compete? Not only is it true, but you can compete on a National Championship level.

Let us introduce you to the lowest-key of all low-key forms of competition: the *postal meet*. The postal meet is somewhat like playing chess through the mail or computer games over telephone lines—you and your opponents never meet face to face. It works on the honor system: you ask someone to be your witness and time you for the event you're going to swim. Then you write your time on the entry form, have your friend sign it, and mail it to a national center where the results are tabulated. A few weeks later, you find out how you did. It's hard to imagine a lower pressure swim meet!

There have been several postal meets held and many of them are popular annual events. Here are some examples: in the *One-Hour Postal Swim*, you swim as far as you can for a solid hour while your friend counts your laps and keeps an eye on the clock. The people who go the farthest in each age group receive medals. In a similar postal race, people kick for ten minutes with no fins allowed. There used to be the *Super Swim*, two swimming miles (3,300 yards) in which the best time wins. There have also been *postal pentathlons*, where you send in your best times from that season's Masters meets in each of the fifty-yard races (one of each stroke) and the 100-yard Individual Medley. Find out through your local Masters swimming organization how to enter.

WHAT, NO TURNS?

Why limit yourself to a pool? Open-water swimming caught on big during the Depression, only to fade into later obscurity. Huge purses were offered as prize money for such seemingly impossible feats as crossing the Catalina Channel. Recent years have seen a resurgence in amateur participation and the La Jolla Rough Water Swim, the oldest continuously held open-water race in the country, is now so popular that they have to divide male and female swimmers of different ages into separate heats. About 1,400 competitors and 10,000 spectators gather for the event. The heats begin in the early morning and continue well into the afternoon.

Take a moment to imagine that you're a runner. After an entire career spent circling indoor tracks, a friend takes you out on a cross-country run. For the first time, you see plants and wildlife as you run, feel the sun on your back and the wind in your face, surrounded by sounds and smells you've never known before. Of course, what runner would be foolish enough to stay indoors all the time, running around in circles on a track? And yet swimmers do something even more boring than that—at least you can talk to someone else when you're running. Open-water swimming is such a special aspect of the sport—whether you compete or just do it for the sheer joy of it—that we've devoted a whole section to it. (See Chapter Nine.) If you find yourself feeling bored and stale in your swimming, perhaps you need to get out into the open more often.

TRI-ING HARDER

There are many ways to compete in swimming. A whole host of new multisport events have appeared. While the enormously popular *triathlon*—an event combining swimming, bicycling, and running—is perhaps the best known, there are many other combinations. If you see a *biathlon* scheduled, that usually means a running and swimming combination. (There's another sport by the same name, the *military* or *Olympic* biathlon that combines cross-country skiing and marksmanship.) Other events, descended from lifeguard examinations, may combine swimming, running, surf-skiing, and rowing or paddle-boarding. A few years ago, one event even had a Ping-Pong tournament as one of its legs!

While these often use open water for the swimming portion of the race, there's no reason why they can't be held in a pool. The *Modern Pentathlon*, an Olympic multisport event that uses swimming, running, fencing, horseback riding, and pistol shooting to recreate a Napoleonic soldier's mission behind enemy lines, has the swimming portion in a pool, and some of the biathlons or triathlons in your area might do this too.

Triathloning is a great way to get in top shape.

BECOMING A MASTERS SWIMMER

If you compete, you have to register with U.S. Masters Swimming so they can keep track of who you are and your age. Anyone over twenty-five can become a Masters swimmer, and some areas have an unofficial category for people from nineteen to twenty-four. Unlike most amateur sports, coaches and professional swimmers are allowed to compete too. (There is also a professional swimming circuit.) Because the Masters division includes amateurs and professionals (and also to keep people from switching back and forth), once you've competed as a Master, you can never compete in the Senior division again. There have been a few people who have successfully petitioned to have this rule waived, but most of us don't even want to think about trying to keep up with those kids! As it stands now, Nationals are only open to swimmers twenty-five and over, but rules have been known to change!

Get an application form from your coach or one of your team's officers. If they can't help you, or you aren't on a team, contact your Local Masters Swim Committee (see Appendix) or write to U.S. Masters Swimming, National Secretary, 5 Piggott Lane, Avon, CT 06001.

Besides your name and address, they will ask for your date of birth, age, and sex so they can keep their records in order. After you send in your completed application and your fee (usually about ten dollars), you will receive a USMS registration number. Write this number on your entry forms when you enter USMS sanctioned events. You may never be asked to show your card, but we recommend that you have it (or a photocopy, if you're worried about it getting wet or lost) with you in case there's a last minute question about your entry.

You'll notice on the membership application that there is a box asking for your team affiliation. This means an officially recognized U.S. Masters team. If you aren't a member of an official team, or don't want to affiliate at the time, write "unattached" in the box.

The Local Masters Team

You may find groups of people training and going to Masters

meets together who still don't constitute an official team. On the other hand, there are official teams that don't have a pool or coach and swim together in name only.

Why all the confusion? From the viewpoint of USMS, there is really only one reason why team affiliation matters—team points, and, by extension, relays. You see, at a big meet like Masters Nationals, team points are awarded for the highest finishers in each event and each age group. Since relay events count for twice as many points as individual events, they're especially important in determining which team gets the prestige—and often a trophy—for winning the meet.

In order to keep all of this under control, rules have been established about what constitutes a team and who is eligible to swim on it. There isn't much involved in being an official Masters team—some paperwork, mostly, and an annual fee. If you want to establish a team of your own, your Local Masters Swim Committee or U.S. Masters Swimming can give you more information.

Team affiliations can cause a lot of friction. For instance, some people will be members of a team near their home, but work out regularly with another team closer to their job. If you are in this situation, you may sense some resentment from the people on the second team when they say, "Well, you swim *with* us—why not swim *for* us, too?"

Likewise, some teams exist only on paper—no pool to work out in, no coaches, nothing but a name—but, at the end of each season, can become a major force at a National Championship because of sheer numbers. They may actively recruit swimmers from other teams and, as you can imagine, this can cause a lot of bad feelings.

If you are affiliated with (meaning registered with USMS as a member of) a certain team, you can't change your affiliation at a moment's notice. There would be total chaos if people could change affiliations for every meet, solely for the purpose of getting on a good relay. You have to swim "unattached" for at least sixty days (meaning you can't compete as a member of any team) before you can compete for team points or swim on relays for the new one. This has to be done officially, letting your Local Swim Committee know that you are "changing affiliation." You fill out a form, sign a statement that at least sixty days have elapsed since the last time you represented your old team, and send in a nominal fee. If you are changing from one LMSC's jurisdiction to another, you should notify both of them.

Finding a Team

The best way to find a team is by asking around. If you're already swimming regularly in a lap-swimming or adult education program, someone at the pool can probably direct you to a nearby group. Ask the lifeguards, the instructors, one of the administrative people, and, of course, the people you swim with.

Other possible sources of information are community bulletins, the weekly activities section in your local paper, and the sports tabloids being given away at local sporting goods stores.

Masters teams come in all shapes and sizes. Some of the biggest operate out of fabulous facilities with fifty-meter and twenty-five-yard pools, locker rooms, and a full-time coaching staff. Others may just borrow the junior-high pool after all the students have gone home.

What should you look for in a Masters team? Perhaps the single most important item is its schedule; the finest club in the world won't do you any good if you can't make it to practice. Some teams have morning, noon, and evening workouts every day while others may be more limited.

While most people wind up swimming with the club nearest to their home that has a convenient schedule, there may be several reasons for choosing a club that's farther away. A club may have a coach who's especially good, a large number of competitors in your age group, or a reputation for having many open-waters swimmers. Shop around.

Big teams can afford to hire good coaches. On the other hand, you may be just another face in the crowd on a big team. The smaller teams can often give beginners better attention, even though the coach may just be one of the swimmers who has volunteered to take the workout that day. Facilities can make a difference, too. If you plan on going straight to work from practice, you'll want a locker room and a heated shower. Serious competitors are often swayed by the availability of fifty-meter pools to train in during the summer-long course season. You might also pay attention to the number of people at workouts. Five or more swimmers per lane can be very crowded, especially if the lanes are narrow and you're all doing butterfly.

There are other alternatives. Some Masters practice with age-group or college teams when they can't find another group that fits into their schedules. Remember, you don't have to be on a team to swim in Masters.

8
SURVIVING YOUR FIRST SWIM MEET

Now that we've got you psyched, registered, and affiliated, it becomes our responsibility to see you through your first swimming meet. Don't worry—you can do it.

PAPERWORK

The first thing you have to do is *enter* the meet. Some meet organizers accept *deck* or *post entries*, meaning that you can enter on the day of the meet, but it's better to enter in advance, especially if it's your first meet.

If your coach doesn't have a *meet sheet* that lists the events and carries information about deadlines and so on, you can write the meet director and request one. (It's considerate to send a self-addressed, stamped envelope—these people work very hard to keep everything organized.)

Read the meet sheet carefully. Where is the meet? What day is the meet and what time does it start? When do warm-ups begin? Will there be a lane set aside or a separate pool for warming up during the meet? Is there a deadline for entries, or will deck entries be accepted?

On your mark, get set . . .

The entry form will tell you how to enter; you may put all the information directly on the entry form or send in special cards. What the organizers need to know is your name, age and sex, your address and phone number, and your team affiliation and *Masters registration number.* Then you tell them which events you are entering, and your best times for each event.

Since you've never swum in competition before, you don't have a best time for any of the events. You could write "NT" or "no time," but sometimes that isn't allowed. Even when it is, you're better off putting down something because of *seeding.* Since more people will sign up for a race than there are lanes to put them in, a race is divided into several *heats.* Seeding is the process of assigning people of similar speeds to the same heat. If you enter "no time," you'll go to the very bottom of the list and be put in with the absolutely slowest swimmers. You may or may not belong in a heat that slow. Entering an accurate time will help you get into the right heat.

How do you get a time? The easiest way is to swim the event at practice one day. Don't do it right in the middle of a workout when you're tired. Give yourself a few minutes' rest first. For an even more accurate time, have someone race you in the next lane—the competition will make you try harder. Then when you have your time, chop a big hunk off it because the excitement at the meet is guaranteed to get your adrenaline going. How much should you chop off? It's hard to say, but five seconds for each minute that your swim just took is pretty conservative. Remember—adrenaline is the stuff that makes little old ladies pick up cars!

Another easy way to come up with an entry time is to ask your coach for advice. Most coaches have years and years of experience watching swimmers at meets, and some of them have an almost uncanny ability to predict a swimmer's time.

Once you've swum your race, of course, you'll have a real time to enter for your next meet.

WHAT EVENT SHOULD I SWIM?

That one's easy: any race you want. The whole idea is participation. If you think you'd like to try something, go ahead.

People will often choose the shorter events, 50s and 100s, for their first meets, but there isn't any reason why you can't swim something longer. As a matter of fact, the 50s and 100s may be the worst place to start because sprinting puts the biggest strain on your heart. If you're worried that you're too old for this sort of foolishness and think you're just asking for trouble letting yourself get talked into racing, go for something longer, like a 200.

Likewise, go ahead and enter whatever strokes attract you. There are technical rules about how the strokes are to be performed, but stroke judges tend to be very understanding when someone's obviously a beginner. Even if you do get disqualified, you've lost nothing. Ask the judge to explain what you were doing wrong so you can fix it. It can be disappointing, but it's not the end of the world. Everybody gets disqualified sooner or later for something. It's part of the learning process.

One last thing. Be sure and write down for yourself what events you entered so that you won't be running around the morning of the meet trying to find out!

GETTING READY

Let your coach know that you're going to swim in a meet. He or she can help you prepare by making sure that your strokes and turns are legal, giving you some tips on race strategy, and fine-tuning your workouts so you're at your peak when the time comes.

You should also take some time to learn to dive off the blocks. Starting blocks don't seem all that high when you stand next to them, but when you get on top of them and look down at the water, you feel like you're standing on top of your house. They're worth practicing on, though. The speed you develop by diving off the blocks can lop as much as three or four seconds off your time. (If you are absolutely terrified of them, you *can* dive off the side or even start in the water; just expect to be looking at the soles of everyone else's feet.)

The question arises: what do I do about my goggles? Nearly everyone practices with goggles nowadays, and you get used to seeing the turn-targets at the end of the lanes clearly. Taking off your goggles when you compete can be very disorienting, so it's a good idea to learn to dive with them on.

Try keeping your goggles a little on the loose side for everyday practice. If you learn to keep them on in practice they surely won't come off when you've tightened them up at a meet. When you do your dive, experiment with your head position until you find the angle that keeps them on. Some experts recommend higher than normal, others say lower. It's whatever works for you. A little trick that helps is to press them gently against your eye sockets just before you start, squeezing some air out to create a vacuum that helps to hold them against your face.

It's a good idea to have everything ready the day before your meet so you aren't running around in a panic the morning of the race trying to find your goggles. Here's a list of must-haves:

A swim suit. Two is a better idea, so you have an emergency spare. The old ones always seem to give out when we're nervous and in a hurry. You can have one ready to slip into after your warm-up so you don't sit around all day in a wet suit.

Your goggles. A second pair, or at least a spare strap, is highly recommended.

Caps, if you wear them. Guaranteed to rip just as your heat is called to the blocks, so bring extras.

A towel or two and something warm to slip into are also recommended.

Then there's a whole list of nice-to-haves like a hat or visor, sunglasses, suntan lotion, a pencil and paper to write down your times, and a stopwatch if you have one. And how about folding chairs, coolers, beach umbrellas, aspirin, and cash for pizza and ice cream afterward! You might also want to bring your camera.

Many people have trouble sleeping the night before a race. Some of us become worried that we aren't really psyched up properly if we *don't* toss and turn. If you have this problem, don't worry. One rough night won't hurt your performance. Swimmers like to say that it isn't how much sleep you had the night before that matters—it's the night *before* the night before!

THE BIG DAY

If you can, find someone with whom you can carpool. Another person's presence will help reassure you. Besides, some of these pools are notoriously hard to find!

Your entry form should have told you when the pool would be available for warm-ups, and you should try to get there as early as possible. You should have had enough experience by now to know that you can't swim well if you haven't warmed up. Racing is the same, only more so.

When you get to the pool, the first thing you'll have to do is check in, letting the meet organizers know that you're there and that you're going to swim the events you've entered. There's usually a table with a big check-in sign and a crowd of people around it.

Find a place for your gear and then get into a warm-up lane with people who seem to be about the same speed as yourself. Don't go jumping into the lane with the human torpedo just because he's the only person there—you'll just drive each other crazy. Ask your coach for a good warm-up. After you've been to a few meets, you'll begin to find out what works best for you. Be sure to build into it, and do some sprints near the end to clear out the cobwebs. Practice the strokes you'll be swimming, get used to the targets at the end of the lane, check that the backstroke flags are still the same number of strokes from the wall, and try to clear up anything else you can think of that might be a problem.

HOW A SWIM MEET IS RUN

A few minutes before the meet begins, the officials will clear the pool. Then the first heat of the first event is called to the blocks by the starter, who sends them off with a pistol or a horn. At the end of the race, the timers write each swimmer's time on a card which is sent to the results table, where it's recorded for determining the awards for each age group. And the next heat is called to the blocks.

Obviously, you have to find out what heat and lane you're going to be in. You may pick up a card with your lane assignment that you take to the timers, or there may just be a list posted. Either way, don't miss your event. If you can't swim your race for some reason, let one of the people at the check-in table know.

After you swim your race, ask the timers what your time was and write it down for future reference so you can use it as your entered time the next meet. If you have a coach or teammate at the meet, ask him or her to write down your split times in the longer races—you can learn a lot about your pacing from them.

RELAYS

Most meets offer relay events, too. While individual events are swum in five-year age groups, relay divisions are in ten-year brackets—25+, 35+, and so on. The age of the *youngest* swimmer on the relay determines the category the team competes in. That way, you can still put together a team if you don't have four people in the same age group.

Since you're never sure who is going to show up at a meet, relays are deck-entered on the day of the meet. If someone asks you to be on a relay, do it! Don't be shy and argue that you're too old or too slow. Relays are great fun and when they say they want you to swim with them, they mean it.

The two standard relays in Masters are the 200 freestyle relay and the 200 medley relay, although you may find others at some meets. The distance refers to the total distance of the race—some people like to call them *four-by-fifty* relays to prevent confusion. Relays are run in all-male, all-female, and mixed (two males and two females) divisions. By the way, the medley *relay* order—back, breast, fly, and free—is different from the *individual* medley relay.

THE EVENTS

Some of the events Masters swimming recognizes are different from other swimming divisions. Here are the official Masters short course events (in yards):

- Freestyle: 50, 100, 200, 500, 1,650;

- Backstroke, Breaststroke, and Butterfly: 50, 100, 200;

- Individual Medley: 100, 200, 400;

- Relays (Men's, Women's, and Mixed): 200 Freestyle, 200 Medley.

The long course events are the same, except the 500-yard freestyle becomes 400-meters, and the 1,650-yard free becomes 1,500-meters.

This is too many events to offer for a one- or two-day meet, so your local meets will only offer a selection. If you watch the meet schedules, you'll see that all the events are offered several times each season.

SOME BASIC RACE STRATEGY

Before we begin a brief look at how to swim the events, we want to tell you the one basic rule of racing strategy:

Swim your own race!

This means that you don't let anyone else set your pace or

your stroke timing for you, but stick to the strategy that you've decided on, letting your body and the way you feel determine how you swim.

General Principles: The best way to swim any race is at a consistent pace. You may have gotten the impression from watching track meets on television that it's better to hold back for a final "kick," but that's because runners can save energy by hanging back in the pack so they don't have to fight the wind. None of the other swimmers can decrease your water resistance in a swim meet, so you're better off budgeting your energy and swimming at a constant pace.

Swimming at a constant pace *feels* as if you're swimming harder and harder as the race goes on, because you are tiring. Many coaches tell swimmers to *build* their races, starting out at a comfortable pace and going faster, but this is to trick them into swimming at a steady pace. Get your splits in the longer races and see if you're holding pace or not. (Take into account that your first split will normally be three–four seconds faster than the rest because of the dive.)

Use the first few strokes of the race to establish your stroke, your pace, and your feel for the water. *Then* start to think about racing. Some swimmers become so nervous or excited that they even forget to breathe!

In a moment, we'll discuss the different distances, but first, let's take a look at each of the strokes:

Freestyle: Most people feel relatively comfortable racing freestyle, probably because we do so much of it in practice. The fastest swimmers may only take two or three breaths in a fifty because breathing slows most swimmers down somewhat. Obviously, you can't do this if it's taking you closer to a minute to swim your fifty, but you can still try to decrease the number of times you breathe. Just don't make the mistake of stopping your shoulder rotation at the same time.

Remember too that the start and the push-offs from each turn are much faster than your swimming speed. Immediately after a start or push-off, don't start flailing your arms around just because you're excited. Wait until you've slowed down to your swimming speed before you start to stroke.

Backstroke: The biggest problem people have with racing

the backstroke is doing the turns. Be sure that you've practiced your backstroke turn during the warm-up; even though the flags are always supposed to be the same distance from the wall, this pool may seem very different from the one you practice in. Remember to count your strokes the same way you do in practice.

Breaststroke: The problem that occurs most often in breast-stroke races is that swimmers "lose their stroke," meaning that their rhythm and feel for the water fall apart. This is usually caused by watching your competition (who can be counted on to have a stroke totally different from yours) or not doing enough breaststroke at *race pace* in practice—when you try to race, it feels all wrong.

Butterfly: Like breaststroke, butterfliers have a tendency to lose their rhythm if they don't do enough fast quality swimming in practice or if they watch their competition while they're racing. There's another problem that occurs in *all* races, but it's especially bad in butterfly—going out too hard. If you swim too fast, you'll go into serious oxygen debt and develop so much lactic acid that your swimming will become extremely painful. Since butterfly is the most strenuous stroke to swim, going out too hard can be especially unpleasant. Make sure you establish your pace, your tempo, and your breathing pattern right from the start in a butterfly race.

The IMs: Individual medleys are especially challenging races to swim because you tire *all* your swimming muscles and because different swimmers have different strong and weak strokes. If someone gets way ahead of you in an IM, don't give up—his or her next stroke may be terrible!

You can't count on your good strokes making up for your weak ones—you have to swim hard on all of them. Here's another tip: start thinking about your turn and the stroke you're changing to *before* you get to the wall, and use your push-offs and glides to really stretch those tired muscles.

Let's turn now to strategies for different distances. As we said in an earlier chapter, your muscles have three different energy systems. We'll look at the distances in terms of which energy system predominates.

The sprints: The 50s and 100s are usually considered to be sprints, but that's because the best swimmers can swim them so fast they rely on the sprinting energy system, which has only enough fuel to last for about a minute. Since many of the people reading this book will take well over a minute to swim 100 yards or meters, we're going to consider the 50s as sprints and save the 100s for the middle distances.

In a sprint, you have to go as fast as you can the whole way. It's as simple as that, but it doesn't mean *thrash*. Be careful to establish your stroke. If you watch the fastest sprinters, you'll see how smooth and powerful they look. Try to get that same feeling. You have to really concentrate up on the blocks so you don't get left standing there. Once you start, take a stroke or two to get your feel for the water and then *build*.

The middle distances: The anaerobic energy system, the one that creates that burning lactic acid, can produce energy for a maximum of two or three minutes. Anything longer than that has to rely primarily on the aerobic distance system. Your middle-distance events will probably be the 100s and the 200s.

Since efforts of this duration produce lactic acid, the middle-distance races are the ones that produce the most intense muscular pain; the sprints are too short, and the longer races force you to swim slower to avoid going into oxygen debt. For many people, this makes the middle distances the most challenging events and hardest to learn to swim well.

The ideal way to swim these races is to swim at a quick but not all-out pace at the start. As the race goes on, you should gradually feel your arms and shoulders burning more and more until you come to the end, right at the point where you can't maintain your pace any longer. If you aren't already feeling the lactic acid building up in the middle of the race, you haven't gone out fast enough.

Your splits will tell you how well you paced yourself. Were you slower in the middle of the race than at the end? That means you were afraid of the pain, and held back too much. Or did you go out too fast and drop dead in the last part of the race? When you hear swimmers say "the piano fell," that's what they're talking about. You were swimming along and all of a sudden you slowed down so much, it looked like a piano must have fallen on your back!

Swimming a good middle-distance race takes a lot of experience—and a lot of courage!

The distance races: In the distance races, you wind up having the same amount of pain as in the middle distances, but you take it in smaller doses over a longer period of time. Most people will be able to swim faster in a meet than they ever can in practice, so it's hard to find that perfect pace. It takes practice, and the good swimmers look at their split sheets as if each were a Rosetta Stone about to unlock deep mysteries.

With experience, you may find that there are certain points in a distance race where you tend to slacken your pace. This may be because of a break in concentration, discouragement ("Oh, no, I'm only halfway?"), or having gone too fast. Get to know your own weak spots in the long races and be on your guard for them. When you get to that point, you can say to yourself, "Here's the time to really concentrate on keeping up my pace!"

9
ROUGHING IT

A brief glance at the artworks, myths, and legends of past civilizations should be enough to convince anyone that water has always held a particular fascination—and a particular terror—for the human species. Psychologists tell us that the deepest layers of our unconscious still feel the tug of the seas from which all life evolved and physiologists have discovered that our bodies, which are mainly water, still respond on the most basic, cellular levels to the daily cycles of sun and moon that direct the tides.

Few runners and cyclists would continue to participate if they were sentenced to spending all their training and recreational time circling a track, yet swimmers rarely venture outside of the pool. When they do have the opportunity to swim in the open, surrounded by the beauty of our planet's oceans, lakes, and rivers, the experience often brings fear rather than exhilaration.

While swimming in open water is inherently more dangerous than swimming in a pool, it is our *fear*, rather than an accurate assessment of the dangers themselves, that keeps us from enjoying swimming in open water. While most of our

Open-water swimming can be very exciting.

fears are irrational and totally out of proportion to the actual risks, we do tend to minimize or totally ignore real threats to our safety.

DEALING WITH FEAR

While we think nothing of hopping on our bikes to pedal over to a friend's house or slipping into our running shoes for a quick jog during the lunch hour, many of us have serious misgivings about wading into a body of open water. And yet, our chances of being hurt or injured while swimming are actually much lower than when we're running or cycling along a roadside.

Part of the thrill and excitement of open-water swimming comes from being in a natural and therefore unpredictable environment. Unfortunately, it can be so foreign that for many it verges on the terrifying. There are two main things that people fear most about open water: being attacked by a creature or being overpowered by the water itself. In either situation, your own fear can be a bigger threat to your safety than the perceived danger.

Animal Attacks

Yes, it is true that sharks, or any other predators for that matter, can be very dangerous creatures. But do bears keep you from enjoying Yosemite, or wolves prevent your hiking in the mountains? Did you know that every year three times as many people die from bee stings as are bitten by sharks? While the chances are much greater that you'll be killed or maimed in an auto accident on the way to beach, or get run over by a powerboat while you're in the water, the danger just doesn't seem as immediate as the thought of some dark, silent shape gliding up from below and having you for lunch.

Just as on land, most creatures in the water are frightened by a human. The more people there are, the fewer other creatures you're likely to find. The yelling and screaming melee in the mass start of an ocean-swimming race probably scares off everything that can move for miles! Areas with heavy shark populations are usually well-known and avoided.

Predators are lazy. If you ever should run into an ocean predator, your best response is the same as when you're biking or running and come across a big vicious-looking dog. Keep going about your business, swimming smoothly and power-fully. Panicking and thrashing around in the water will make it appear that you are sick or injured, and that's what predators look for—an easy dinner. If they don't lose interest, an aggressive movement may convince them you're going to be too much trouble. The Navy recommends you strike a shark on the end of the nose as a last resort. Let's hope none of us ever gets close enough to take that advice.

Some things that lie on the bottom can cause problems—sea urchins, stingrays, and a few rare poisonous fish—but most often people hurt themselves on rocks and debris. It's a good idea to wade out, shuffle your feet, and check the bottom conditions, especially before dashing into the water at the start of a race.

Some ocean-dwellers, like jellyfish and plankton, have no means of propulsion. They're bobbers and floaters and it's *your* job to stay out of their way. They can sting very badly. Even though we're talking mostly about *creatures*, we'll throw in kelp, seaweed, and seagrass too, since some people are afraid of becoming entangled and getting pulled below the surface. The same rule applies—don't panic. It only makes things worse. All you have to do is clear the area around you by pushing gently with your hands.

Being Overpowered

Swimming in very rough water demonstrates nature's awesome power as clearly and immediately as a thunderstorm or earthquake. Distances seem much greater over water; swim a hundred yards from shore and you can feel incredibly small and insignificant. This feeling alone can be very uncomfortable for some swimmers, and there are always tales of swimmers being swept to sea by an undertow or the tides.

Actually, few currents pose any real danger if you stay calm. If you remember that you can float no matter where the water takes you (no, undertows do not tow people under) and you can swim *across* any current, no matter how strong it is, there's little to be afraid of. The only real danger is that you'll exhaust yourself before you get to shore. Keep in mind that you should never fight a current by swimming directly against it. Again, don't panic. Just swim at your normal pace across the current until you are free of it.

The current that causes the most problems for people swimming in the ocean is the *rip*, a place where the water brought in by the surf tends to concentrate as it returns back to the sea. Rips can be surprisingly powerful, and coastal lifeguards are constantly having to rescue people who were caught in one. It's not really that the rips are dangerous. It's just that many swimmers don't know that rips are usually only a few yards wide and don't extend very far away from shore. If you find yourself being carried out to sea, just swim parallel to the shore for awhile, and you'll get clear of the rip.

If you stand on the beach and watch, you can see rips forming. They're marked by a streak of murky, foamy water that extends out from the beach and fans into a brownish semicircle past the surf line. This is where the water churned up by the surf is concentrating as it returns to sea. If you watch a lifeguard rescue someone in a rip, you'll see that he or she goes right out through the middle of it; the current helps the lifeguard get to the swimmer faster. Sometimes, you can use this same technique to your advantage in the start of an ocean race.

One current you should be concerned about, though, is the tidal current sometimes found in a large bay with a narrow inlet. The enormous amount of water moving in and out of San Francisco Bay as the tides change, for instance, can cause currents under the Golden Gate several knots faster than the fastest swimmers can swim, and they can extend very far out to sea. While your best bet is to plan ahead for such emergencies, if you get caught in one of these, just remember to angle across the current and conserve your energy.

Rivers pose a different aspect of this same problem. You can always swim across the current to the shore, just as you would do in the ocean, but what if there are violent rapids ahead? You may not have time to get to the shore. You can swim at a 45-degree angle, across the current and back against it at the same time, but you should not be in this situation in the first place. If you are swimming in a river, scout ahead and see what's downstream.

Surf can be frightening, too. The best way to learn to deal with surf is to watch how other people do it, diving under waves, or jumping high enough that the wave's force passes under them. Once you get the hang of it, playing in surf can be great fun. You might even learn to bodysurf!

The one thing you need to remember any time you are caught in a powerful current is that *exhaustion* is the biggest danger. If you keep a cool head and swim across the current rather than fighting it, you'll swim your way free.

THE REAL DANGERS

While our unrealistic fears of being attacked or swept out to sea tend to cause panic which can then become a very real threat, there *are* dangers that open-water swimmers need to be aware of. Unfortunately, our reactions to these *real* dangers are usually recklessness and nonchalance.

The one thing that you should be concerned about any time you swim in open water is the possibility of *hypothermia*, a life-threatening drop in your body's internal core temperature. One of the first things to go when a person's body temperature begins to fall is *judgment*, so you need to take precautions in advance.

How cold is too cold? You'll have to find out from your own experience, but any time the water is below sixty degrees Fahrenheit, hypothermia is an *immediate* danger. From sixty–seventy degrees, one should be very concerned, and temperatures in the seventies can even present a danger, especially if one is out of shape and in the water for a very long time. There are several precautions one can take, the first of which is to practice swimming in cold water. With repeated exposure, your body will begin to shunt blood away from your skin, keeping it down below the surface so that your heat isn't drawn off as rapidly. This form of stress-adaptation is called *acclimation*.

You can also insulate yourself to some extent. Your body loses a great deal of heat through your scalp, and most ocean swimmers wear not one, but two swim caps to help hold in heat. That second cap makes a surprisingly big difference, especially if you can manage to trap an insulating layer of air under it. Larger goggles that cover the entire eye socket can help prevent discomfort, too.

A few swimmers will wear a layer of grease—usually petroleum jelly, sometimes mixed with lanolin—for extra insulation. It tends to wash off after awhile, but it certainly helps reduce the initial shock of extremely cold water. If you grease up, have someone else spread it on you, and don't put it past

James "Doc" Counsilman (right), past U.S. Olympic coach and English Channel swimmer, joins another swimmer for some early-morning training.

your knees or elbows. That way you won't smear your goggles when you adjust them, even if you have to massage a cramp in your leg or foot. Another form of insulation, but one that we can't really recommend unless you're planning a real marathon swim, is a layer of *fat*. Some manufacturers have come up with wetsuits designed specifically for swimmers. Check your local scuba or swimming store.

Another danger that people don't take as seriously as they should, is *powerboats*. Not only should you wear a cap for insulation, it should be brightly colored for visibility. Those of us who ride bikes a lot know that drivers in cars often don't see us. We can promise you that people in boats are definitely not watching for swimmers, and even with a brightly colored cap you are only a speck in the water.

The danger of behavior that may result in a broken neck is also taken much too lightly. Every year, swimmers and surfers are paralyzed by diving headfirst into unfamiliar water and hitting their heads on rocks or sandbars. Many of these tragedies could have been prevented by following a few simple rules. Don't ever dive headfirst into the water or under a wave—always have your arms extended in front of you. Check the bottom carefully in your area for sandbars or large rocks before you take any chances playing in the surf. And when you're surfing, avoid falling headfirst off of a wave into the shallow water in front of it. Exit by pulling back and letting the wave pass under you if at all possible.

OPEN-WATER SWIMMING TECHNIQUES

Now that we've helped you get a little better grip on your fears of open water and pointed out a few things worthy of your respect, let's get out there and have some fun. Just as cross-country running or off-road cycling require different sets of skills from their more domesticated counterparts, swimming in open water presents some new challenges to the pool swimmer.

The best way to train for open water is to get out there and practice in it as often as you can. The more often your body is exposed to the cold, the wider the variety of conditions you experience. The more times you face your fears and phobias and realize how greatly they're exaggerated, the more confident you'll be and the more fun you'll have.

The first thing you'll notice is that there are no lane lines! How are you supposed to swim in a straight line without them? This is something that you can work on in the pool. Swim a length with your eyes closed and see if you can make it to the other end without hitting a lane line. (It helps knowing how many strokes you take per length so you won't be tempted to peek.) There are lots of little stroke irregularities that can throw you off; ask your coach or another swimmer to help you find the problem. You may be failing to push all the way back on one side, twisting your head as you breathe, pulling too deeply with one arm, or a whole host of other things.

But even the straightest swimmers will be thrown off course by shifts in currents and wave action. The solution is knowing how to *look*. There are several ways to do this: looking at the beginning of your breath as you raise your head, after your breath before you put your face back in the water, or even between breaths. Experiment and find what's most comfortable for you. You can practice this in the pool, too, and the more practice you get, the stronger your neck muscles will be. Raising your head is hard work.

Alternate breathing is a big help, too. If you only breathe on one side, you won't be able to see the course markers in an around-the-buoys race that goes to the other side. If you can breathe on either side, you have the flexibility to breathe away from wind or chop no matter where it's coming from.

Another thing people often do to help themselves swim in a straighter line is have a friend accompany them on a paddle board. This makes it very easy—you let them worry about steering while you just swim alongside. You can save a lot of energy by not having to lift your head and look every few strokes.

Open water is rarely as calm as the water in a pool, even during the most crowded workout when everyone's swimming butterfly. You'll find that making a conscious effort to bring your elbows higher on your recovery and roll your shoulders more will help keep your arms from catching every wave that comes by. Swimming in rough water requires an unusual ability to know when to relax and let the waves do what they will, and when to fight it. No one can tell you this beforehand. It depends on your stroke, your own strengths and weaknesses, and the conditions you're swimming in. Once again, there's no substitute for getting out there and learning by doing. Just make sure that you *never* swim alone, especially if you are a beginner. It's a good idea to ask the lifeguard to keep an eye on you.

If you swim in salt water, you'll be a bit more buoyant because of the water's increased density. The main reason you kick is to support your legs, and since the salt water is already helping here, you can conserve energy by kicking less.

If you're near the ocean, it's also a good idea to practice going out and coming back through the surf. Why not learn to bodysurf while you're at it? It's great fun and you'll never forget the first time a wave carries you so far in that it leaves you on the beach. It's an excellent technique to know for racing in the ocean, too, and swimmers can often gain several places over their competitors in the last few yards of a race.

You can get pretty spoiled being able to stand up on the pool

Be sure to take precautions against the cold when swimming in open water.

bottom to clear your goggles or hop out onto the pool deck to massage a charley horse. Out in the open, you've got to be able to do these while you either float or tread water.

Another technique that's very helpful is training yourself to keep water out of your mouth. Many of us allow a little pool water to rinse in and out of our mouths at times, and this is a very bad habit for open water. Even the most remote mountain streams show signs of pollution these days, and water in more populated areas can be a nightmare. Swallowing is definitely not recommended. Salt water can also irritate a person's tongue to the point that marathon swimmers have occasionally had to abandon major swims because swallowing became impossible.

We should give you one last warning. Once you've developed a taste for swimming as far as you want with no turns or lane lines or other swimmers getting in your way, passing through schools of brightly colored fish, watching exotic landscapes pass beneath you, and feeling energized from the chilly waters and the power of the sea, you will have discovered perhaps the biggest hazard of open-water swimming—*addiction!*

10
SURVIVING YOUR
FIRST OPEN-WATER
RACE

In the last chapter, we gave you some tips for making your first forays into open water more pleasant and enjoyable. We also introduced you to some of the special techniques such as learning to swim in a straight line, how to "look," and dealing with the cold and various other rough-water conditions.

Sooner or later, you'll have an opportunity to enter an open-water race. In fact, many people who are now veteran ocean swimmers did their very first long open-water swim in competition rather than recreationally. If you have some experience under your belt beforehand, that's even better.

Just as swimming in the open requires different techniques from those used in a pool, so do open-water races call on different skills than those needed in meets. This difference is wide enough that some people are much more successful at open-water competition than in pool meets, just as certain people seem naturally gifted for a particular stroke.

TYPES OF RACES

Open-water races generally fall into four categories: the

You'll be handed anything from a tag to a popsicle stick with your place number as you "enter the chute" to finish your race.

Some open-water swims are so popular that heats by age and sex can continue throughout an entire morning!

Don't stand there expecting a wave to go around you! Try dolphining underneath instead. Grab onto the sand if you need to and then you can come up swimming.

If race rules permit it, bring along your own paddler to help you along.

Check out the course map before you jump in. You'll want to know which way to round those buoys.

Be sure to be at the site in plenty of time to sign up.

coastal or *shoreline* race in which you enter the water, swim parallel to the beach, and exit in a different place; the *triangle* or *around-the-buoys* race in which you swim around a closed course marked by floats or buoys; the *out-and-back* race in which you swim out around a buoy, the end of a pier, or a similar marker and return; and the least common, the *crossing*. Although races are sometimes held across very small lakes and bays, most crossings are either solo marathon attempts or the relay races we'll discuss later.

Promoted race distances are notoriously unreliable, and are usually (though not always) inflated. Because conditions are so variable, records (course records, and your own personal best times) are pretty meaningless. Currents, surf conditions, added buoyancy and low tide that makes you run farther on the beach can all affect your times. If you swim a course several times in practice, you can find an extremely wide range between your best and worst times in just one season.

Also be aware that even if the course is precisely the advertised distance and the conditions are perfect, your time still may not bear any resemblance to your pool times. Properly executed flip turns, for instance, can take one whole second apiece off the time it would take to swim the distance in a straight line. This means a swimmer with good turns can swim 1,650 yards more than a full minute faster (a second for each of sixty-five turns) in a pool than in open water. So take all of it—times, distances, records—with a grain of salt.

PREPARATION

Preparation is the key to a good open-water race. Practice swimming in a straight line, looking, and keeping your elbows high. If you can't get out in open water, you can still practice all of these techniques in a pool.

If at all possible, get some experience swimming in open water before your race. The more comfortable and confident

As this start of the annual La Jolla Rough Water Swim shows, competitors have plenty of company—and beautiful scenery—at the start of the race.

you feel, the more fun you'll have and the better you'll swim. Use the buddy system—take along an experienced friend who can help you get started on the right foot by showing you how to deal with rips and surf and so on. Don't be too shy to ask. Most open-water swimmers are glad to have someone to swim with, even someone slower and less experienced. They love to see someone else get hooked!

Look for a race with a good reputation for your first experience. Talk with your teammates and ask them if they can recommend a good race for beginners, one that's short, well-organized, and fun. Some locations—especially lakes and sheltered areas—have warmer and calmer water than others. Other races may offer something special afterward, like an all-you-can-eat barbecue or a local festival.

Aside from a recommendation that you abstain from alcohol for a few days because it can throw off your body's heat-regulation system, there's little else you need to do the days before your race besides eating well and getting plenty of sleep. You may hear people talk about *carbo-loading* before a distance race. Carbo-loading is an advanced technique that's only appropriate for top-caliber athletes in serious competition, and even then the practice is questionable and can cause serious problems. On the other hand, if your teammates invite you to carbo-load the night before, they're usually just looking for a kindred spirit to share some pasta.

For most athletes, it's enough to maintain a diet that's consistently high in complex carbohydrates. Don't overeat the night before your event and avoid spicy foods or fats. Rely on high-carbohydrate foods that you are familiar with and enjoy.

The day of the race, eat a small, bland meal of about 500 calories several hours before your event. It's not necessarily because you can't swim right after eating; it's just better to have an easy digestion well before the race. Oatmeal is an old standby. Heavy grains, milk products, or butter nauseate some athletes. Also, recent studies show that sugar taken immediately before an event can hamper performance. (Your body responds to the sugar by secreting insulin, which interferes with your ability to use your body fat for energy. You are therefore forced to rely more on muscle glycogen and will burn it up faster.) Sugar ingestion in dilute amounts during exercise, however, won't interfere with your body's use of fat, because once you start exercising, you suppress the release of insulin.

Finally, remember that plenty of water is essential to maximize performance. You won't be able to drink at regular, frequent intervals as you might in a cycling race, so try *hyperhydrating* the night before, particularly for a long ocean race. Also drink about one quart of water about an hour prior to performing, and eight–sixteen ounces a half hour or less before your race. For pool races, a reasonable amount of water consumed before and after your events will probably suffice.

If you're feeling anxious about your safety, the cold water, or staying on course, consider asking someone to paddle for you, if the rules allow it. Try to go out and practice with your paddler before the race so he or she will know which side to be on, how close to stay to you, and what your stroke looks like so he or she can find you in a mass start that may include hundreds of other swimmers.

RACE DAY

Get started in plenty of time. You'll be amazed at how many people show up for these races, and parking is usually a problem. You've got to park the car, unload all your stuff, and get in line to check in before the deadline. If you're a "beach entry" because you didn't advance register, allow yourself even more time.

Most races require you to wear a brightly colored cap for your own safety. You might want to mark yours with a felt-tip pen so that someone watching from the beach (or your paddler!) can see you better. This is especially considerate if someone's concerned about your welfare. Remember to keep your cap on after the race until you're sure you've warmed back up.

Put some petroleum jelly on your underarms, the insides of your thighs, and along the back of your neck and shoulders. Chafing always seems to be more of a problem in open water, and these are the places that it's most likely to occur. (Remember, it will also help to insulate you.)

Talk to other people who've swum the course before. There

may be a trick they've discovered or a tip they can give you that will help you swim better. Even if it's something as minor as knowing that there is usually a cold spot in a certain location, and that it's usually about so many yards wide, can ease your mind when you get there. Surfers, lifeguards, and fishermen can be very helpful sources of information, too.

Be sure that you understand what the course is. Some of them can be quite complicated, especially the around-the-buoys courses, and it would be a shame to be disqualified because you passed on the right of one of the markers when you were supposed to be on its left. Unfortunately, the terminology can sometimes be confusing. Does "pass the second buoy on the right" mean the *buoy's* right, or *your* right? If the course is at all complicated, the race organizers should post a map somewhere or put one on the entry forms.

Take a close look at the area where you'll be starting. It's a good idea to go out and swim a short warm-up unless the water is extremely cold. You'll have a chance to check the bottom conditions and the surf and plan where you want to start. Does the bottom drop off slowly or steeply? How far will you be able to run? Is the bottom smooth and sandy, or rocky? Are there any sandbars or obstructions right where you are planning to run? A warm-up will also help work off some of your nervousness.

Watch the water conditions. Races are usually held early in the morning when the water is calmest—most waves are a result of wind, which in turn is caused by the sun's heating of land and sea—but there may still be some surf. Plan your start well in advance. If there are any surfers around, watch how they handle going out through the surf and coming back in.

If the finish area is nearby, go over and take a look at it. Try to imagine how it will look from the water as you're coming in. If the finish is going to be somewhere else, find out what it will look like. How far will you have to run up the beach? What is the bottom like there? (If it's rocky, you want to swim as far as you possibly can before you stand up.)

Listen to any announcements. There may have been a last-minute course change, or they may be telling you how to identify the markers, or explaining how the start or finish will be run. If they're using a white flare to signal get ready and a red one for go, it's nice to know which is which!

The Start

Don't start in the middle of the pack unless you're a veteran water-polo player and ready for a lot of kicking and pulling and shoving. For your first few races, stay over near the sides of the pack and you'll have a much more pleasant experience.

Here's a trick that will help you get the best possible start. Keep your eye on the starter and watch the gun. Go when you see the *flash*. Light travels so much faster than sound that you'll get a big jump on the people listening for the bang.

The principle behind a good open-water start is to *run* as far as you can. You've probably noticed that people casually strolling on the pool deck are walking faster than you can swim. Don't start swimming until the depth has slowed you to your swimming speed. If you dive under a wave, you'll have to decide whether to get back up and run, or keep swimming. The same thing goes if you are swimming and come to a sandbar. Should you get up and run? Sure, if it's shallow enough!

The Race

The first few yards of the race will be a madhouse of arms and legs, and it will be very difficult to settle into a rhythm unless you've started out on the very edges of the pack. Don't get upset, just keep a cool head. It will all sort itself out in a few more yards.

Try to settle into your pace as soon as you can. Some people make the mistake of swimming really hard to try to get warmed up, only to go into oxygen debt and have to slow down. (Be especially careful not to do this if you are swimming in an icy mountain lake at high altitude.) Others, especially those who didn't warm up, will try to start out slowly, using the first part of the race for a warm-up. They may never get warm!

What usually happens when the water is chilly is that you feel cold at first, but after a few minutes you don't notice it any more. The cold causes some numbness which can be a blessing or a curse. The blessing is that you don't feel how cold you are or how sore your muscles are becoming. The curse is that you lose some of your feel for the water—all the more reason for trying to practice with perfect technique at all times.

One technique that can be of great value is knowing how to *draft* another swimmer. Bicyclists, stock car drivers, and speed-skaters all do it—so can you. Since you're moving through water as opposed to air, drafting takes effect at much slower speeds. (Thank goodness!) An object moving through the water drags some of the water along behind. If you can get into water that's already moving forward, you can save a lot of energy, but you have to get pretty close for it to work. (Be careful not to jam a finger hitting against the person's feet; this can result in a very unhappy draftee!) But if you see a faster swimmer passing close by, you might try and hitch a ride for a while. You might even plan ahead of time to take turns drafting off and on with a teammate, as bicyclists do.

But note that drafting *is* controversial. While most races don't specifically forbid it, many people still feel there's something vaguely unethical about it. Open-water swimming has a kind of one-person-alone-against-the-elements romance about it and drafting seems a little like cheating. On the other hand, if the person you draft turns out to be a bicycle racer, he or she may think you're cheating if you don't let *him or her* draft *you* after a while!

A reliable support crew can help in open-water races.

Drafting behind a boat is quite clearly illegal, and triathletes please note: drafting on the *bicycling* portion of the race is strictly prohibited in nearly all triathlons.

Be careful not to just blindly follow another swimmer, assuming that he or she is going in a straight line. You'll see people going every which way, and in very long races, the pack can spread out until it's several hundred yards wide. You just have to look where you're going, and hope that everyone else is also off course. Remember that you can switch to breaststroke for a moment to look around if you're really disoriented, or roll over into your backstroke to look behind you.

The Finish

Eventually, you'll see the flags marking the finish. The same rule of thumb holds true for the finish as for the start: running is faster than swimming. A good way to judge is to swim in until your fingers can touch bottom—that's about the right point. Of course, if the bottom is covered with rocks or mud, you may decided to swim as far as you can.

Your legs may feel very rubbery, especially after a long swim. Kicking extra hard the last few yards as you're coming in will help wake them up. Triathletes find a little breaststroke kick just before the finish especially good for preparing their legs and ankles for the bike.

Open-water races usually end on the beach in a *chute*, a funnel-like arrangement laid out with flags or banners. Newcomers often make the mistake of thinking they've finished once they've come out of the water—only to lose several places on shore. You still have to run up the beach and through the chute. Someone may hand you a marker (usually a tongue-depressor or popsicle stick) with a number on it. Take it to the table near the end of the chute and the people there will record your name and age group. That's all there is to it. Give yourself a pat on the back. Congratulations are in order!

Afterward

After you've made sure you've been checked off at the finish line, it's a good idea to go back into the water and swim an easy warm-down. The cold may prevent you from realizing how hard you actually swam and many people are surprised at how stiff they are the next day. A little warm-down can prevent a lot of soreness.

You should get dried off and into your sweats, even if you don't feel cold, and remember to keep your cap (or caps) on until you are quite sure that you've warmed back up. Drinking a warm beverage from a thermos, or having some food that's been kept hot in a thermos can make you feel much warmer in a hurry.

Don't be too concerned about where you finished or what your time is when you're just starting out. Swimming in open water is a very different sport from pool-swimming, and it takes time and a lot of practice to get the hang of it. Concentrate instead on enjoying yourself and learning from the experience.

A VERY SPECIAL OPEN-WATER EVENT

Many swimmers think open-water relay races are the most exciting and enjoyable swimming events held. Although there are all sorts of variations, a typical relay race might go like this: you have six people and a boat on each team. One person starts from shore and swims alongside the boat. After a certain interval, usually half an hour, the second person jumps into the water and tags the first swimmer. The first swimmer gets into the boat, and after another half hour, the third person jumps in to replace the second one, and so on. After the first time through the rotation, the interval usually will change to ten minutes for the second and all subsequent legs.

We'd like to encourage you to participate in one of these races if you ever get the chance. Spending the day on the water with your teammates cheering each other on, comparing notes, and coaching each other, while getting in there once in a while to do *your* bit, is wonderful fun. These relays often seem to be held in some of the most beautiful places on the planet—Lake Tahoe, San Francisco Bay, the Maui Channel, just to name a few. Maybe you should organize a team of your own!

THE ULTIMATE CHALLENGE?

Legend says that the Ironman all began over beer at an award ceremony—who was the fittest athlete, the winner of the Waikiki 2.4-mile Rough Water Swim, the two-day, 112-mile Around-Oahu Bicycle Race, or the 26.2-mile Honolulu Marathon? It was finally agreed that the *ultimate athlete* would be the person who could do *all three*—within twenty-four hours! Doing that would take a real "Ironman."

Thus was born the fastest-growing participant sport of the decade, the *triathlon.* Professional races with cash awards have appeared, and there's even talk of trying to make it an Olympic event.

Unfortunately, all the hype and hoopla tends to drown out the fact that you don't have to be a super-jock to get in on the fun. Forget what you've seen on television with people collapsing in agony. Most triathlons are *much* shorter races than the premiere event, the Hawaii Ironman Triathlon, and men and women of all ages, from all walks of life, compete and have a great time. After all, how serious can they be taking it when they refer to a shorter race as a *Tinman?* If you join one of these events looking for fun, that's what you're likely to find.

You may not realize it, but being a swimmer with open-water experience is a valuable asset. Because swimming relies more heavily on technique than the other two sports, you have an advantage over the runners and cyclists who are new to swimming. All you have to do is get your legs, knees, and ankles in shape—they have to learn to swim. If you're tempted to give a triathlon a try, go for it!

There are lots of other multisport events that include swimming as one portion of the race, too. Biathlons are quite popular, usually combining swimming and running. Another way to get in on the excitement is as the swimmer in a triathlon *relay* (one swimmer, one biker, and one runner combine their talents).

The ultimate challenge for a triathlete, however, may be finding the time for training!

EPILOGUE: A LIFETIME OF FITNESS AND FUN

For many of us, our swimming workout is one of the few moments in the day when we can get a little perspective on our lives, easing our everyday cares and concerns with rhythmic, aerobic exercise and feeling satisfied at seeing our own steady improvement. The water cleanses us inside and out.

Swimming is a great lifetime sport, but like anything that we do daily, there's always a danger that it will become a routine chore rather than something we look forward to with excitement and enthusiasm. We hope that you've found many ways to keep your swimming interesting and challenging, whether your goals are just improving your fitness, exploring open water, or participating in competition.

The great secret to making your love for swimming last a lifetime lies in keeping yourself challenged. Set goals for yourself, asking, "What do I really want from swimming?" Armed with the information and suggestions in this book, outline a plan for meeting those goals quickly, efficiently, and enjoyably. Each goal achieved becomes a step on the way to even bigger goals; each disappointment, a spur to try even harder next time. The joy, the confidence, and the equanimity we achieve spills over into all areas of our lives, making us healthier, happier, and more human.

See you in the water!

APPENDIX I:
SAMPLE WORKOUTS

The workouts in this section are based on the information in Chapters Four, Five, and Six, which you should refer to if you don't understand the terminology being used or have any questions about *why* a particular workout is structured as it is. Our sample workouts all add up to 1,650 yards, the *swimmer's mile*. Don't be discouraged if this is too far or not far enough for you. Take a look at the examples and modify them to suit your own needs and desires. You can swim more or fewer repeats, make each swim shorter or longer, bring in extra sets or leave some out. Be creative!

We've also chosen to use *rest* intervals instead of *send-off* intervals to make the goal of the workout sets clearer, because it's the amount of rest in between swims that determines what sort of a workout you are getting. When you actually swim with several people in a lane at once, you will probably use a send-off interval to keep everyone synchronized.

DISTANCE TRAINING—OVERDISTANCE
AND SHORT REST SWIMS

If you have been lap-swimming, this is probably the type of swimming you've been doing all along. Distance training keeps the heart rate within the Target Heart Rate Zone as much as possible, stressing the aerobic energy system, and training the body to consume fat along with carbohydrate as the main fuels. Let's assume that this is what you've been doing for your three-times-a-week workout:

WORKOUT 1

1,650 yards of freestyle; straight swim

Boring! Let's break it up a bit, while still keeping the main portion of the workout as overdistance training:

WORKOUT 2

Warm-Up:
 4 × 100 free; descend @ 30-second rest interval (RI)

Main Sets:
 5 × 50 kick @ 15-second RI
 800 long, slow distance (LSD)

Warm-Down:
 200 free easy

That's more interesting, isn't it? The warm-ups and warm-downs help decrease the chance you'll hurt yourself or be stiff the next day, and we found a chance to slip a little bit of kicking in, too. And the 800 LSD will still give you an opportunity to "mellow out" and do your overdistance training. Let's try another variation:

WORKOUT 3

Warm-Up:
  400 free; take only two breaths every fourth length

Main Sets:
  8 × 100 free, "pace," @ 15-second RI
  Kicking ladder—25, 50, 75, 100—10-second RI; do one of each kick, your choice which

Warm-Down:
  200 LB, breath 3, 5, 7, 9

Workout 3 is very similar to 2, except we've made the 800 LSD an 800 "broken" for fifteen seconds at the end of each hundred. This gives you a chance to look at the clock and see if you are "holding your pace." We threw in a ladder for fun on the kicking—you get to choose which kick you'll swim for which distance. And to add a little more variety, we've added some breath control at the beginning and a "lung-buster" at the end, in which you breathe every three strokes the first fifty, every five the second fifty, and so on.

QUALITY MIDDLE-DISTANCE WORKOUTS

These always take a little longer to swim, because you are resting more between swims. The goal in these sets is to stress your anaerobic system as well as your aerobic one, to concentrate on swimming with your best technique, and to get used to the feeling of lactic acid accumulating in your muscles.

WORKOUT 4

Warm-Up:
 200 swim easy
 150 kick
 100 pull
  50 swim hard

Main Set:

3 × { 100 easy, followed by 30-second rest
     100 build, 20-second rest
     100 all-out sprint, 10-second rest

Warm-Down:
 100 free easy
  50 back easy; s-t-r-e-t-c-h your arms
 100 free easy

One problem that many people have, especially those who have done nothing but LSD training, is that they don't know how to swim *fast*. When they try to sprint, their stroke falls apart. The idea behind the main set in Workout 4 is to swim the easy 100 with your very best form, then increase your speed in the second 100 while hanging onto your good form, and then swimming the last 100 as fast as you can without letting your stroke fall apart. Your heart rate should be well above your THR Zone after the last 100.

A QUALITY STROKE WORKOUT

Too much overdistance training in the "specialty" strokes, butterfly, backstroke, and breaststroke, can cause serious problems because these strokes depend so much on correct *timing*. If you swim 400 yards of breaststroke, your rhythms will be totally wrong for a 50-yard sprint. For this reason, many coaches prefer to use freestyle for most of their distance training, and save the other strokes for quality workouts so that the swimmers practice the strokes near race pace.

WORKOUT 5

Warm-Up:
    100 free easy
    100 kick, your choice
    100 free pull
    100 free build

Main Sets:
    $5 \times$ $\begin{cases} 50 \text{ breast; descend @ 30-second rest} \\ 50 \text{ free easy @ 30-second rest} \end{cases}$

    $3 \times$ $\begin{cases} 100 \text{ free, pace, @ 15-second rest} \\ 50 \text{ kick, your choice, @ 15-second rest} \end{cases}$

Warm-Down:
    300 free easy

In Workout 5, the first main set is aimed right smack at swimming a good middle-distance specialty stroke race. On the easy fifty freestyles in between, you can swim as slowly and easily as you want. They're just there to help your body recover and rest, and get ready for the next fifty stroke. We specified breaststroke here, but you could do any of the strokes (including freestyle!) for this workout. It's very important that you descend, swimming faster from one fifty to the next.

Sets like this are very grueling when done correctly, taking lots of determination and guts to keep swimming harder as you start feeling the lactic acid building up. We've followed the main set with a "pace" set of freestyle so that you can shift gears and get in some distance training, too. Two big quality sets may be too much for one day.

Remember what we said about not doing two heavy quality workouts on successive days. When you start introducing more quality swimming into your training, you have to be especially alert for *overtraining*.

◉

A SPRINT FREESTYLE WORKOUT

The sprinting energy system is the primary source for efforts under one minute and is stressed by allowing long recovery times in between short maximum efforts. Because these recoveries take so long, sprint workouts tend to be shorter in total yardage than middle-distance and distance workouts. This workout is only 1,350 yards, but may take longer than any of the other sample workouts, which are all 1,650 yards.

WORKOUT 6

Warm-Up:
200 free easy
100 kick
100 free build
4 × 50 free, descend @ 20-second RI

Main Set:

6 × { 25-yard free sprint, from a dive
15-second rest
25 free easy
rest until heart rate is under 100 (or even 90!)

2 × 75 KPS (kick, pull, swim), your choice, @ 20-second RI

Warm-Down:
3 × 100 easy

You may have noticed that this workout has a longer warm-up. It's extremely important that your body is fully prepared for all-out sprinting. A good way to accomplish this is to swim your normal warm-up and then follow it with some extra building or descending swims that will bring you up to speed, as we've shown in the warm-up above. If you find that you still don't feel right, don't hesitate to do some extra warming up. You'll also notice that the warm-down is longer, for the same reason. Sprinting is hard work!

INDIVIDUAL MEDLEY (IM) WORKOUTS

What we said about being careful not to do too much overdistance work in the specialty strokes also holds for the individual medley. IM workouts are usually divided up into many smaller swims so that you can maintain proper form for each of the strokes.

Most IM workouts are based on the normal order of strokes in the individual medley race: butterfly, backstroke, breaststroke, and freestyle. Memorize it.

Because the turns from one stroke to the next are such an important part of the race, coaches like to design workout sets so that you are doing at least two of the strokes, with the turn between them, in each repeat.

WORKOUT 7

Warm-Up:
> 200 free easy
> 100 IM kick
> 50 free build

Main Sets:
> 12 × 75 IM rotation @ 30-second RI
> 4 × 50 kick, your choice down/freestyle kick back, @ 15-second RI

Warm-Down:
> 200 free SLRS (swim, left arm, right arm, swim)

The "IM rotation" in the main set means that you swim the first ¾ of a 100 IM—that is fly, back, and breast—for the first seventy-five. Then you swim back, breast, and free for the next seventy-five. Then breast, free, and (back to the beginning) fly for the third seventy-five, and free, fly, back for the fourth one. You continue "rotating" through the IM order like this until you've done twelve repeats.

There are lots of possibilities for designing workout sets based on the individual medley. Here are some suggestions:

- *125 IMs*—you swim two lengths of one of the strokes and one length of each of the others. You can rotate around, with two lengths of fly on the first one, two lengths of back on the second, and so on, or you can always do two lengths of the same stroke.

- *Fifties*—you can swim a set that's just part of the IM, for instance, one length of fly and one length of back. Then you could do another set that's all fifties made up of breaststroke and freestyle, or back and breast.

See if you can come up with other variations of your own.

DESIGNING YOUR OWN WORKOUTS

All of these workouts are intended to give you an idea of how workouts are put together and show you how many possibilities there are for variety—even a 400-yard warm-up can be made interesting. We'd be very disappointed to find that anyone had just taken these seven workouts and done nothing but use one of them each day.

Be creative. If you think about what you are trying to accomplish and how to do it, you should be able to make up your own workouts that are fun, challenging, and beneficial.

Even if a coach gives you a workout every day, you can use the ideas you've found here to make your coach's workouts more challenging. For instance, if he tells you to do 10 × 50, your choice, you could use one of the IM rotations we showed you, or descend them in groups of three, or alternate a fifty of hard swimming with a fifty easy, and so on. The possibilities are endless. There's no excuse for boring workouts. If your coach gives you a boring workout, make it your responsibility to turn it into an interesting one!

APPENDIX II:
MASTERS
SWIMMING—WHO TO
CONTACT

UNITED STATES MASTERS SWIMMING INC.

President:

Michael A. Laux
8 Myrtle Avenue
Westport, CT 06880
(203) 226-3392

Vice President:

Verne H. Scott
646 Elmwood Drive
Davis, CA 95616
(916) 752-0690

Secretary:

Dorothy Donnelly
5 Piggott Lane
Avon, CT 06001
(203) 677-9464

Registrar:

Enid Uhrich
Box 5039
Sun City Center, FL 33570
(813) 634-7564

Treasurer:

Reg Richardson
915 Flore Vista Drive
Santa Barbara, CA 93109
(805) 962-5812

Zone Committee Chair:

Gail M. Dummer
Department of Health &
   Physical Education
Michigan State University
East Lansing, MI 48823
(or)
1202 Red Oak Lane
East Lansing, MI 48823

ZONES

Colonies Zone:

Jeanne Mason Bostwick
3 Golden Hill Court
Catonsville, MD 21228
(301) 465-9611 (work)
(301) 744-1504 (home)

Dixie Zone:

Peter Mullen
Box 4743
Brenau College
Gainesville, GA 30501
(404) 534-6279 (work)
(404) 536-8470 (home)

Heartland Zone:

William Tingley
2008 Trevilian Way
Louisville, KY 40205
(502) 585-2201 (work)
(502) 451-4567 (home)
(502) 454-3029 (sec'y)

Breadbasket Zone:

E. Kevin Kelly
1400 Dean Avenue
Des Moines, IA 50316
(515) 265-3497 (work)
(515) 967-2414 (home)

Cow & Oil Country Zone:

Karen Barnes
12317 Teakwood Road
Edmond, OK 73034
(405) 771-3086

Continental Divide Zone:

Edie Gruender
3329 N. Valencia Lane
Phoenix, AZ 85018
(602) 946-5805

Oceana Zone:

Dore Schwab, Jr.
Box 772
Ross, CA 94957
(415) 456-5945

Southern Pacific Zone:

Kurt Mosso
(805) 961-4044 (work)
(805) 967-0597 (home)
Steve Scofield
(818) 885-8082

INDEX